MULTICULTURAL PLAYS

A Many-Splendored Tapestry
Honoring Our Global Community

by Judy Truesdell Mecca

Incentive Publications, Inc.
Nashville, Tennessee

I would like to thank my daughter, Jensen Trice Mecca, for help with this collection of plays. When I wrote my first book for Incentive Publications, she was one year old, and helped me by taking regular naps, allowing me time to work. Now, at age ten, she's a terrific writer herself, and a wonderful, bright girl who helped me with research and gave me valuable ideas and criticism. Thanks also to my husband, George Mecca, for everything. Lucky me!

Illustrated by Gayle Harvey
Cover by Gayle Harvey and Marta Drayton

ISBN 0-86530-411-4

Table of Contents

Overview of
Multicultural Plays

Honoring our Global Community

The earth is made up of a rich cultural mix of people. Each different ethnicity brings a colorful variety to the world—and here is a collection of plays honoring some of these cultures.

Each play is under thirty minutes in length. Each offers opportunities for several cast members to have speaking parts, as well as opportunities for groups that can be modified depending upon how many boys and girls you wish to include. Suggestions for props, costumes, and scenery are included for each play, but with something extra! A song, a craft, a recipe—a little peek into the country or people portrayed. Some of the plays are set in modern times and deal with current customs, and some are based on time-honored folk tales shared around the fire on an African night, or in an Iroquois long house in the dead of winter.

Each group of people, then, is like a beautifully colored, richly textured patch in a quilt. Whether you're celebrating your own heritage or learning a little bit more about another, these high-spirited plays will provide your group of young people a unique opportunity to learn and honor the variety of cultures that exist in our world.

At the beginning of each play, you will notice a play heading page and a cast page. You may wish to use these pages to create templates on which to base play programs. These programs are a wonderful way of providing your audience (and your actors!) with keepsakes of the performances.

TWO BEAR TALES

A Play Based on
Native American Folk Tales

TWO BEAR TALES

CAST

Iroquois Chorus

Word Weaver

The Children, including:
Running Deer
Laughing Stars
Little Eagle
Red Fox

Bear

Wind

Coyote

Snowflakes

Ice

Turtle

Raccoon

The Turtle Family, including:
Turtle #2
Turtle #3
Uncle Bert Turtle
Cousin Mervin Turtle
Aunt Myrtle Turtle

TWO BEAR TALES

Notes to the Teacher/Director

Storytelling has always been an integral part of the Native American culture. Long ago, in many Iroquois long houses, young people would gather around elder relatives or visitors, begging for tales. They would refer to the older person affectionately as "Uncle," and he in turn would call them all "Nephews," whether or not they had any blood in common. Winter was the true time of storytelling—indeed, tales in warm weather were forbidden by custom. It is not hard to imagine the origin of that particular custom—in warm weather, boys and girls could go outside and play!

Two tales involving a favorite Native American folk character, Bear, are combined in the following play. In one, Bear is outwitted by Coyote who tricks him into freezing off his tail in the frozen lake. In the other, Bear's friend Turtle uses his large family to defeat Bear in a race, and to teach him a lesson about being unkind to his friends.

This play offers a wide variety of opportunities to include larger groups of boys and girls. It begins with a song, sung by the Iroquois Chorus, which can be a large choir of the whole grade—or an Iroquois duet! You have flexibility in the number of Children who gather to hear Word Weaver's tales. Lines are written for four actors, but these can easily be combined to feature only one or two "Nephews," or divided among more boys and girls than just four. (It might be fun for the class to think of their own Native American names to replace the ones offered, or to add to the list if other actors are included.) The Snowflakes can be one actor or many, and several students can team to portray the "Ice." (See Scenery.) The Turtle Family can also be expanded or made smaller. Lines are written for five little Turtles in addition to the main character Turtle, but again you have great flexibility. At least five additional Turtles are needed to convey the essence of the joke Turtle plays on Bear, but the number can certainly be expanded, depending upon the space you have in your classroom or acting area. And, of course, various animals can be watching the race and cheering on Bear or Turtle. In fact, young actors not ready to read or memorize lines quite yet can easily be included as Snowflakes or race spectators if you would like to include more than one age group.

A little more information . . .

Early Iroquois Days

The Iroquois Indians of North America were a remarkable people. As early as the 16th century, the Iroquois had formed a league of five Indian nations. Men representing each tribe served the people. Fifty male sachems, or chiefs, met. (The sachems were chosen by women, who were the heads of family clans. In Iroquois days, women were very well respected.) The members of the council tried to persuade each other with their carefully chosen words. All decisions had to be agreed upon unanimously. Some American historians believe that the government of the United States is patterned after this form of government, where each tribe, or state, keeps its own identity but belongs to a larger nation.

Today we use the name Iroquois to refer to this tribe of Native Americans, but their original name was **Haudenosaunee** (ho-din-no-SHAW-nee), which meant "people of the long house." This name described these people well—many huge families lived in houses up to 150 feet in length. As many as twenty families, all of whom were related in some way, might live together in one house.

In the Iroquois nation, the men did the hunting, but the women did most of the farming. They tilled the fields around the villages, and planted corn, beans, and squash. The Iroquois held festivals to give thanks when the crops became ripe. One of these was the Green Corn Festival, when the people gave thanks and praise to the Creator for their good harvest. In the winter, they celebrated a festival called "The Most Excellent Faith." This was a time of cleansing of the spirit and indeed, the homes! They would clean their own homes, then visit their neighbors and stir the ashes on their hearths. They gave thanks to the Creator for keeping them safe for another year.

The Iroquois had no written language, so the art of storytelling was extremely important to them. The sachems were responsible for remembering the history and important stories of the tribe and passing them on. They had a little bit of help— beads called wampum, which were used in a kind of picture writing. The main method of recording and sharing stories, however, was the spoken word.

You may have heard of an Iroquois warrior named Hiawatha, who spoke out in favor of peace. Hiawatha became an advocate for peace after a long period of suffering. After the deaths of his wife and three daughters, Hiawatha went to the woods to live alone. He became known as something of a hermit by his people. He lived in the woods until another Iroquois, Degandawida, approached him. Degandawida needed Hiawatha's help to communicate ideas about living in peace to the other Iroquois. Degandawida had a speech impediment that prevented him from speaking effectively. Hiawatha joined with him to travel from tribe to tribe offering a message of peace and unity.

MAKE A STORY RATTLE

The play begins with the Iroquois Chorus singing about their "story rattle"—a rattle used to summon people to listen to a tale. Perhaps your class would like to make story rattles to shake during the song. Each member of the chorus—or perhaps each of your students—can make his or her own to take home. Here's how:

Get a dowel rod, branch, or other stick and make sure it as smooth as possible. Take two disposable, picnic-style bowls, made out of materials like Styrofoam or cardboard, and about six inches in diameter. Put large beans or beads between the bowls, then staple or glue the edges closed, with the beads or beans trapped inside. Now cut two opposite holes along the edge of the bowls and stick your dowel rod through until about an inch or so protrudes from the top. Using masking or other strong tape, secure the bowls around the pole so that the stick will not slide in and out of the bowls, and the beans or beads will not escape.

Now to decorate! First, paint the bowls in some Native American design and let them dry. Then wind some brown yarn around the handle (the long end of the rod), solidly covering it. Leather strips would be even better if you can find them. Attach some strips of leather or yarn (about six to eight inches in length) to the short end of the rod, so that they swing free when the rattle gets a shake. Attach beads to the ends of your strips. If you can get some feathers from the craft store, attach one or two at the base of the bowl and at the top to cover your masking tape. Give it a shake! Story time!

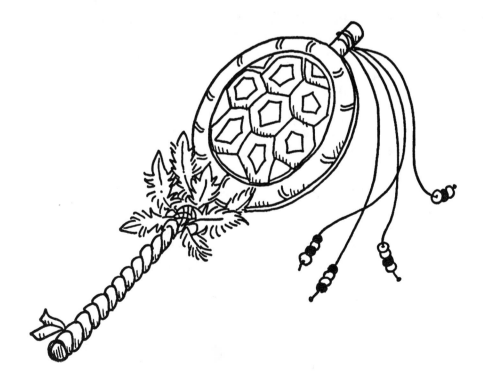

TWO BEAR TALES

Props

- Story rattles, if you choose to use one or more during the Iroquois Chorus song

- A pile of fish for Coyote. Use plastic toy fish, stuffed plush fish, or fish that your class has made out of construction paper.

- Some white substance to represent the snow and frost that fall on Bear while he sleeps. Let your cast help you decide—will it be tiny paper circles from the hole punch? (They always end up on the floor anyway!) Or packaged white plastic snow? Cotton balls? Christmas tree tinsel (either a glittery garland or the kind that simulates icicles)? Steer your class away from glitter; although it would create a pretty shiny look, it could easily go in actors' eyes. (You might use blue or white theatrical make-up available at craft and party supply stores.)

Scenery

This play requires little scenery, but affords you and your cast an opportunity to have fun and be creative.

Word Weaver needs a chair or stool on which to sit, stage right.

You can employ great creativity to suggest a frozen pond. You might want to dress a string of children, in light blue or white or a combination (or maybe in T-shirts with "Ice" or "Lake" written in marker, or on little signs hanging around their necks). They could kneel with their arms linked drill team style, blocking the audience's view of Coyote's paw, for instance, when he fishes. Maybe one student has a pouch or backpack on his or her back, out of which Coyote pulls the fish. Then, shortly before Coyote returns to wake up Bear have a member of Ice stick up his or her hand and grab hold of the tail, holding fast until the tail comes off. The Turtle race would work the same way—all Ice members would be on their knees, tightly packed, so that neither Bear, nor the audience can see multiple Turtle family members hiding, ready to pop up.

Another way to represent the icy pond using a smaller number of youngsters would be to have them paint a long roll of butcher paper to represent the frozen lake, then have two or three students support it, depending upon its size. One of those students can stick up his or her hand from behind the "paper lake" and grab hold of Bear's tail in a way that is similar to that described in the above paragraph. It might be funny to have the whole Ice ensemble move about two feet to their left (with little steps) when Coyote leads Bear to "another part of the lake." The Turtle Family could also creep in and hide more easily behind paper than their fellow students.

Depending upon how many children are involved (and how noisy your butcher paper is!), you may wish to direct the boys and girls who represent the frozen lake to stay in place between the time of Turtle's challenge and the actual race. Just position your initial Turtle Family scene farther stage left of the lake, or at some other part of your classroom or acting area.

You'll need something to represent the tree behind which Coyote hides and the two oaks that represent the finish line when Bear races Turtle. These can be chalkboard tree drawings, students dressed in brown pants and green tops (again, perhaps with "Tree" written on their chests), or trees cut from art board and painted. Of course you can always have Coyote pantomime a tree when he is hiding behind it, and let the audience members use their imagination.

Costumes

The actors in the play who portray people (as opposed to bears, coyotes, etc.) can dress as modernly or as traditionally as you and your cast would like. You may wish to investigate the traditional dress of the Iroquois or other Native American tribes, and represent it as closely as possible. Or you may wish to suggest a traditional costume. It might be fun to unify the Iroquois Chorus by having them all bring T-shirts from home. Dye the T-shirts light brown and then fringe the sleeves and bottom of the shirts. Your class can add beads, if they like, to some of the fringes and knot the strands to hold the beads in place. They can decorate the rest of the T-shirts as they wish, with fabric markers.

Word Weaver should look older—perhaps he can wear a longish gray wig (yarn can be used in a pinch) pulled back in a pony tail or braid. You may wish to be completely authentic in his clothing, or costume him in modern attire with a headband or Native American blanket. The play does not specify whether the children are modern or long-ago "Nephews." This is up to you and your group. If you choose modern, let them run offstage to get sweaters and jackets. If you go a more traditional route, they need to add blankets and costume pieces that will represent skins.

The animal costumes provide many opportunities for creative thinking. Of course you can purchase patterns and entreat parents to sew costumes out of fake fur, but there are other ways to create fun costumes with less expense and time commitment. For instance, dress Bear all in brown—a brown sweats outfit would be ideal. Cut some bear ears for him out of construction paper and affix them to his head with bobby pins, a plastic bandeau, or piece of elastic. (Make sure his ears are secure—he's really got to run hard!) All animal noses can be made by cutting a single egg holder from a cardboard egg carton. Paint Bear's nose brown and attach slender pieces of elastic with staples, then add brown or black pipe cleaner whiskers. Of course, Bear must have the all-important tail! Various materials will do—a long piece of fake fur, a shiny belt, a doubled over piece of flannel or velour, or even a piece of construction paper if you don't have too many dress rehearsals. The ideal way to affix it (if it's made of sturdier material than paper) would be with Velcro, but a good strong piece of doubled over masking tape should work also. (Don't forget to cross white adhesive tape across his behind after the tail has been frozen off—this could also be used to mask the Velcro.)

Multicultural Plays

Students may wish to help decide upon a costume for Wind. Should it be something solid white, perhaps, such as a leotard and tights outfit, with some piece of white or light blue gauzy fabric or netting as a stole? Should she cover her hair with a white turban or other head covering? Your actress might like to apply white make-up to her face with light blue make-up on her cheeks.

Coyote's basic outfit, sweats or jeans and a T-shirt, should be some combination of tan, gold or gray. He needs a "pointier" nose than Bear—perhaps you can experiment with adding yellow or gray construction paper to the end of his egg carton nose. His tail should be gray and bushier than Bear's—perhaps made of gathered-up netting or soft foam, available at fabric stores.

Your Snowflakes will, of course, be dressed in solid white—leotards and tights, sweats, tutus—whatever they would like and parents are willing to gather. A few sequins and glitter would add a frosty touch, but be sure they are glued firmly in place. Would the Snowflakes like to make themselves little crowns out of cardboard or pipe cleaners and decorate them with some of the same materials used to frost old Bear?

As mentioned in Scenery, you should dress your Ice actors in some combination of light blue and white. It might be fun to dress them in blue jeans and white T-shirts with "Ice" written on their T-shirts with markers. Maybe they would all like to apply white make-up to their faces or dust their hair with baby powder or use a can of white hair spray. (Be careful not to use this product near fire—some brands are inflammable.)

Green hooded sweatshirts will work perfectly for Turtle and his family, and, if they match, will help create the illusion that they're all the same Turtle when tricking Bear. Then, the Turtle Family members can add accessories to make each look different, such as earrings and glasses for Aunt Myrtle Turtle, etc. Shells are not required, but if you would like to make them, try using soft foam. (The Turtle Family should be able to laugh themselves onto their backs and roll around without ruining their costumes.) To do this, purchase large pieces of soft foam from the fabric store. Cut each foam piece into a large circle. Cut a very small pie-shaped slice out of the top of the circle. Use contact adhesive to re-attach the foam where the pie-shaped slice was removed. You could also punch holes in the area around the slice and lace the foam piece up like shoes. This will cause the flat circle to "pooch" up and create the look of the curved shell. Then paint the back of the "shell." The best kind of paint is floral spray, because it is made to use on foam. Cut a small slit in the foam at arm level and loop pieces of twine through to tie around your actors' arms and hold the shell in place. Or, you might save lots of time by simply purchasing plastic trash can lids, punching holes at arm level and threading a slender rope through.

16

IROQUOIS CHORUS

(See music page 28)   COME AND HEAR MY STORY RATTLE
COME AND LISTEN TO MY TALE
LISTEN, HEAR MY STORY RATTLE
COME AND HEAR THE TALE I TELL

GATHER AROUND, THE FIRE IS GLOWING
AND THE GROUND IS WHITE WITH SNOW
WINTER WINDS AROUND US BLOWING
BENDING BRANCHES TO AND FRO

COME AND HEAR MY STORY RATTLE
COME AND LISTEN TO MY TALE
LISTEN, HEAR MY STORY RATTLE
COME AND HEAR THE TALE I TELL

(WORD WEAVER, the story teller, enters and takes his seat far stage right. Boys and girls cluster around him, sitting on the floor, eager to hear a story.)

Running Deer   Oh please, Word Weaver! Would you tell us a story today?

Laughing Stars   Yes, yes, Uncle! A story, please!

Little Eagle   It's been far too many moons since we have heard any story from anyone! Please, Uncle, please!

Word Weaver   *(Holding up his hand for silence.)* My little Nephews, you make a storm cloud between my ears with all your begging! I cannot tell a story today!

Red Fox   Why not, Uncle! We have finished all of our chores!

Word Weaver   Today is a warm day, Nephews. I have told you many times what will happen if I tell you a story on a warm spring day!

Running Deer   *(Dejected)* Hornets will leave their nests and give us a sting.

Little Eagle   Snakes will sneak into our beds and surprise us! *(Little Eagle scares a nearby child)* Hiss . . . hiss . . . *(the child squeals.)*

Laughing Stars   And all the bugs in the world will buzz around and make us itch!

Word Weaver   This is so! Now run and play outside in the fields, Nephews, and come back for a story when it is winter!

(The CHILDREN exit and, out of the audience's sight, put on sweaters or other warm coverings such as blankets. While they are gone, WORD WEAVER speaks to the audience:)

TWO BEAR TALES

Word Weaver And I will have a few moments' peace . . . while I decide on the perfect tale to tell them!

(The CHILDREN re-enter and sit back down in the same spot.)

Red Fox How about now?

Running Deer Now it is really truly winter, Word Weaver, dear Uncle, and we need to be out of the cold HEARING A STORY!

Word Weaver A story, you say?

Children *(Ad-libbing)* Yes! Yes, please!

Word Weaver Hmmm. Let's see. I might know one or two . . . perhaps a story about our old friend Bear?

Children *(Ad-libbing)* Yes, yes! We love Old Bear! Tell us the story!

Word Weaver Let me see if I can remember the tale. Oh yes, the tale of the tail! Perhaps you have noticed, Nephews, that the old Bear has a very little tail. In fact, you can hardly see his tail at all. But that is not the way it always was! Once, many springs and winters ago, Friend Bear had a long, shiny, black tail. He was very proud of it and liked to swish it around just to impress his neighbors.

(Enter BEAR, center stage, proudly displaying his tail, turning his back so that the audience can see it, etc.)

Now, one day, when Hatho, the Spirit of Frost, had painted the land white with snow and ice, Bear was walking along, thinking of nothing much except his tail and finding some honey . . .

Bear I sure do wish I could find some honey! But at least I have this beautiful tail!

Word Weaver When who should come rushing up to meet him but our friend, Sister Wind!

(Enter WIND, dancing and swaying and running up beside BEAR.)

Wind Helloooooo, Bear!

Bear *(Shivering)* Brrr . . . that must be my friend, Wind!

Wind Yes, Brother Bear, it is I, Wind! How do you find yourself today?

Bear How do I find myself? Am I lost?

Wind No, Brother Bear, I mean how are you? Are you well?

Bear Oh, yes, Wind! I am very well! If only I could find some honey, everything would be perfect!

Wind At least you have that fine tail!

Bear It is a honey, isn't it!

Wind No, it isn't honey, it's a tail! And a fine one!

Bear Wind, you are confusing me. I am on my way to visit my good friend Coyote. Goodbye!

Wind Bear, wait! I do not think you should go visit Coyote.

Bear Why not?

Wind Because he is not such a good friend to you as you think!

Bear I do not believe you, Wind. How can I believe someone who flies around and disturbs the tree branches all day? Someone who never works or hunts? Coyote is my friend and I am going to see him.

Wind Hear me, Bear. I fly here and there and I see many things! And I tell you that, one day, I will whistle in your ear. On that day, you will know that Coyote is not your true friend! He will trick you! But if you will not listen, I will blow away. Now goodbye!

(WIND and BEAR exit in different directions.)

(COYOTE enters and begins to catch fish.)

Word Weaver Bear should have listened to Wind, Nephews, because she is wise. Bear went straight to see his friend Coyote, who had cut a hole in the ice and was pulling fish out of it as fast as he could.

TWO BEAR TALES

(BEAR enters and approaches COYOTE.)

Coyote (to audience) Ah, look who comes here! It is Old Bear, with his fancy tail! I am so tired of hearing about it! My tail is beautiful and gray—his tail is nice, but it is nothing special. I think I feel a trick coming on . . .

Bear Yoo hoo! Coyote! My, my, look at all the fish you have caught! You will not be hungry all winter!

Coyote My dear friend, Bear! How funny that you should walk up just now!

Bear What should I do, fly? I am a bear, not an eagle!

Coyote I mean, I was just thinking about you, and wishing that I had a long, beautiful, talented tail like yours!

Bear Oh, Coyote, thank you! It is beautiful, isn't it?

Coyote Oh yes it is! (Turns his back briefly to BEAR and rolls his eyes.) Here is what I was thinking. I am forced to use my paws to catch these fish—and I am doing pretty well, as you can see—but what if I had a skilled tail like yours?! I could catch enough to last the whole winter and into next spring!

Bear I could use my tail to catch fish!

Coyote What a good idea! Why didn't I think of that!

Bear Do you think I could?

Coyote Indeed! I have tried it with my own tail, but it isn't . . . nimble . . . like yours! It is so bushy, it is hard to control.

Bear Yes, I have noticed that about your tail. Though it is pretty and gray, it lacks a certain . . . I don't know . . .

Coyote Oh Bear, don't trouble yourself to think. Let's just go to a fresh part of the lake and you can fish!

Bear A fresh part of the lake? But I want to fish right here, in this spot! There must be hundreds of fish right here!

Coyote Oh no, Friend Bear. I have caught every fish in this portion of the lake. Come with me.

(COYOTE leads BEAR to a different part of the "lake.")

Coyote Here we are. Bear, do you think that you could punch a hole in the ice with your mighty fist?

Bear Of course I can!

(BEAR pantomimes punching a hole in the ice.)

Coyote Perfect. Now turn around . . .

(Turns BEAR around)

Coyote And put your tail in the lake until a fish nibbles it. Then jerk it out! You will have all the trout and perch out of the lake in an hour!

Bear Will it hurt when the fish nibble?

Coyote Hurt? Such a mighty tail as yours? You are too funny, Brother Bear! Why, you will hardly feel it!

Bear Then how will I know when to jerk out my tail?

Coyote Hmmm, let's see. I know! I will hide over there behind that tree and watch you. When I see your tail dipping slightly down into the water, I will shout "Pull up, Bear!"

Bear Are you sure you do not mind?

Coyote Oh no, Bear. I consider this an honor. Now sit ever-so-quietly . . . Don't make a sound or you will scare the fish away. Do not even think fish thoughts, or they will know you are here! In fact, see if you can clear your mind of any thoughts! *(To audience)* This will be easier for Bear than for most!

Bear No thoughts . . . nothing about fish . . . nothing about trout or perch . . .

Coyote I will be right over here! Good luck!

(COYOTE crosses over to the tree and peers out for a few moments. BEAR sits quietly.)

Word Weaver So Old Bear fished with his tail and tried to keep his mind empty. The tricky old Coyote watched for a minute or two—then sneaked back to his own home and went to sleep.

(As WORD WEAVER describes this action, COYOTE acts it out, and exits, laughing silently to himself and the audience, holding up the 'shhh!' sign as he creeps out.)

Old Bear sat . . . and he sat . . . and he sat. Pretty soon, he fell asleep. Along came the wise Wind, who tried to wake up her friend Bear!

Wind Bear, wake up! You have been tricked, just as I said! Bear!

Word Weaver But Bear was sound asleep. So Wind gave up, and whistled in Bear's ear. *(WIND whistles in BEAR's ear.)* Snow covered him. Frost formed on his fur! Still he did not wake up.

(SNOWFLAKES tiptoe in and join WIND in covering BEAR with "snow" and "frost." Then SNOWFLAKES exit.)

Wind *(Shrugging)* I tried! *(She exits.)*

Word Weaver Pretty soon, yawning and stretching, the sneaky Coyote returned!

(Enter COYOTE, who acts out the things WORD WEAVER describes.)

He spotted Bear sound asleep, his tail still stuck down in the ice, and he began to laugh and laugh. He pointed and laughed some more. He went over to Bear and said the one thing Bear was waiting to hear . . .

Coyote Bear! Pull up!

(BEAR and COYOTE act out the following action as WORD WEAVER narrates.)

Word Weaver Bear woke up. He whirled around. He tried to pull his tail out of the hole in the ice—but guess what, Nephews! There was no longer a hole there! The ice held his tail firmly; it was frozen solid. He pulled and tugged, but the ice would not let go. Finally, he gave a mighty yank—and off came the tail, stuck in the ice forever. Coyote laughed and pointed and ran away, delighted by the great trick he had played on Bear.

(COYOTE exits and BEAR chases after him angrily.)

Word Weaver And do you know what, Nephews? To this day, bears are not fond at all of coyotes and sometimes, deep in the woods, you can hear a bear moan, sadly mourning his lost tail.

(From offstage, BEAR moans loudly.)

Red Fox *(Snuggling close to someone)* I think I heard him just now!

Word Weaver It could have been our friend Bear—or it could have been the wise Wind, sadly reminding us to listen to good advice.

Laughing Stars That wasn't enough, Uncle! Another story, please!

Little Eagle Please, please Word Weaver! You said you might know one or TWO!

Word Weaver Did I? Did I say I knew two stories?

Children Yes, yes, you did! Another story please!

Word Weaver Well, I do happen to know one more.

Red Fox I knew it. Grown-ups always know one more story.

Word Weaver It is about old Bear again. He never learns his lesson.

Running Deer What did he do this time?

(Enter BEAR, walking along, and TURTLE, sticking his head out of the ice on the lake. BEAR has an "X" of bandages on his rear end where his tail had been.)

Word Weaver Bear was walking along thinking about the trick Coyote had played on him, when he came upon his old friend Turtle. Turtle was in the lake, sticking his head up through the ice.

Bear Hello, Friend Turtle! Are you going anywhere today?

Turtle Hello, Bear. What do you mean 'am I going anywhere?' As a matter of fact, I am going to see my Aunt Myrtle, who is feeling ill!

Bear Oh, I am sorry to hear that. But, Turtle, you are moving so slowly, I wonder if you will ever reach your Aunt Myrtle's house! I thought you were just floating along enjoying the day!

 **TWO BEAR TALES**

Word Weaver Bear had much to learn about what is kind to say to a friend and what is not.

Turtle Bear! Why do you insult me so? You are always teasing me about how slowly I move. At least I still have my tail!

Bear *(Aside, to audience)* Bad news travels fast.

Turtle Hush up now, Bear, and leave me alone.

Bear All right, Turtle, I will see you later. Of course I will, because you will still be in the exact same place when I come back!

Turtle That's it, Bear! That is one insult too many! I challenge you to a race!

Bear A race?! But Turtle, how can you ever hope to win a race with me?!

Turtle Never mind, friend, never mind. Just show up right here, at this very spot tomorrow morning. I will swim under the frozen ice and you will run alongside the lake and we will see who gets to the two oak trees first!

Bear Are you sure you want to look this foolish, Turtle?

Turtle Yes, Bear, I am sure. We will see who is teasing whom at the end of the race!

Word Weaver And with that, Turtle turned and rushed away.

(BEAR exits, and TURTLE turns and exits very slowly.)

Turtle *(Aside, to audience)* This is as much rushing as I ever do!

(TURTLE exits.)

Word Weaver The Turtle may have been slow, little Nephews, but he had two big advantages over Bear. For one thing, he had a wonderful, large family.

(Enter TURTLE FAMILY members, who sit in a circle around TURTLE stage left, while he pantomimes outlining a plan to them.)

Word Weaver For another, he was clever enough to hatch a sly plan and get all of his family members to help him outwit old Bear!

(The TURTLE FAMILY members laugh silently and roll around with mirth at the plan TURTLE has hatched.)

They were wonderful and supportive—but sometimes they laughed a little too hard and rolled onto their backs. This was not good.

(The TURTLE FAMILY members have now rolled onto their backs, and are unable to get up. TURTLE, who is standing, extends a hand to all of them and they exit, slapping each other on their backs affectionately.)

Everyone spent a nice evening, resting and getting ready for the big race. The next morning, Bear and Turtle met at the lake as planned.

(Enter BEAR, RACCOON, and TURTLE.)

Bear It's not too late to change your mind, Turtle! No one will make fun of you if you back out now! Except me, of course!

Turtle Bear, you just take your place and get ready to run as fast as you can.

Word Weaver Sister Raccoon gave the signal . . .

Raccoon On your marks . . . get set . . . GO!

Word Weaver And the friends were off.

(As WORD WEAVER speaks, BEAR seems to be running as fast as he can, straining and looking over at TURTLE, but the actor playing BEAR actually runs in slow motion. TURTLE begins the race with his head visible, then ducks it below the ice and disappears.)

Word Weaver Never has any bear run as hard and fast as our friend did that day! He made his legs pump hard and harder, he seemed to claw the air with his paws! He looked over at his friend Turtle—and saw, to his amazement, that Turtle was ahead!

(TURTLE #2 sticks his head out from his post ahead of BEAR.)

Turtle #2   Hey friend Bear! Hurry up!

(TURTLE #2 disappears below the ice.)

Word Weaver   What poor Bear didn't realize was that he had been outsmarted once again.

Turtle #3   *(Sticking his head up from a hole in the ice farther ahead yet)* Hi ho, Bear! You're falling behind! *(He disappears below the ice as well.)*

Bear   How can this be? Has he been pretending to be slow all these years just waiting for this day?!

Word Weaver   Bear was running so hard and gasping for breath so much, he didn't even notice that Turtle looked just a bit different each time he saw him. Once he looked a little like Uncle Bert Turtle . . .

Uncle Bert Turtle   *(Sticking his head up from a hole in the ice farther ahead)* Hurry up, Bear! It looks like you are losing! *(He disappears below the ice as well.)*

Word Weaver   And the next time he looked somewhat like Cousin Mervin Turtle . . .

Cousin Mervin Turtle   *(Sticking his head up from a hole in the ice farther ahead)* Bear?! Are you going anywhere or just waiting for spring?! *(He disappears below the ice as well.)*

Word Weaver   He ran and ran, thinking that his poor lungs would explode from such hard panting, but when he got to the two oak trees, there was dear Aunt Myrtle Turtle who had made a remarkable recovery from her illness!

(AUNT MYRTLE and RACCOON enter between the two oak trees.)

Aunt Myrtle   Give it up, Sonny Boy, you're history!

(RACCOON holds AUNT MYRTLE's hand up, pantomiming that she is the winner.)

© 1999 by Incentive Publications, Inc.
Nashville, TN

Word Weaver   Bear was so sad and mad . . . and really, really tired . . . that he crept away to his cave where he slept for months and months until spring warmed the world and brought the new buds on the trees. And to this day, bears hibernate all winter . . . just in case any turtles should challenge them to a race.

(As WORD WEAVER narrates, BEAR hangs his head and sadly trudges offstage to his cave. When he has exited, all TURTLES come out and dance around happily, laughing and clapping each other on their backs.)

The Turtles were all very pleased with themselves, not only because they had taught Bear a lesson about teasing his friends, but because they had reminded themselves how wonderful it is to have the support of a big family!

(As WORD WEAVER has been concluding the tale, his little audience has drifted off to sleep.)

Well, look at this! I guess these warriors only needed two stories today. Thank you very much for coming. Shhh! Be very quiet when you leave. Goodbye!

(The CHILDREN wake up and take their places for the curtain call, along with the rest of the cast, who either call "Goodbye" to the audience or reprise the Iroquois Chorus song from the beginning, whichever your little warriors would prefer.)

Come and Hear

Words by Judy Truesdell Mecca

Music by Jenifer Truesdell Christman

Kongjee and Patjee
A Korean Cinderella Story

Multicultural Plays

Kongjee and Patjee

CAST

Kongjee

Father

Doki, Father's new wife

Patjee, Doki's daughter

The Black Ox

First Sparrow

Second Sparrow

Third Sparrow

Governor

First Groomsman

Second Groomsman

The Sparrow Chorus

People of the Village

Villagers Who Perform The Farmers' Dance

Kongjee and Patjee

Notes to the Teacher/Director

We celebrate the rich and colorful heritage of Korea with *Kongjee and Patjee, A Korean Cinderella Story*. It is based on a combination of several versions of this well-loved folk story, which is told in various countries around the world. In every telling, Kongjee (who has other names in other versions of the story) is good and kind and, following the death of her gentle mother, is ill-treated by her new stepmother and step-sister. She keeps her spirits up, however, and ultimately marries the Governor . . . or Prince . . . or Magistrate, depending upon the version. In several versions, Kongjee ends up in Heaven with her mother by climbing a rope up to the clouds!

In many Korean folktales, relatives who have passed away may take the form of animals to protect their loved ones. In our play, it is implied (through the red ribbon) that Kongjee's deceased mother is working through the Black Ox and the Sparrows to help Kongjee out of difficult situations. When Doki accuses the Black Ox of being "some tokgabis," she means that he is an evil spirit, capable of trickery. This kind of spirit is sometimes referred to as a doggabis.

There are four different groups, which can be as small or as large as you would like to accommodate the number of children who wish to participate. Three of the Sparrows have lines, but there can be as many Sparrows as you like. The same is true of the People of the Village, the Farmers' Dancers, and the Governor's Groomsmen.

As with all the other plays, you can costume the play traditionally, or in modern dress. Whichever you choose, be sure to include hats for the farmers with long white ribbons attached to the top, which will twirl as they dance. The Farmers' Dancers can, of course, be dressed as elaborately or as simply as you like.

In almost all versions of this story, the Governor rides up to Kongjee in what is called a palanquin—an elevated box supported on long poles by Groomsmen. You may have seen it referred to as a "sedan chair." Of course, if you have a talented parent who would build this for you, it would be wonderful to include. Increase the number of Groomsmen by two and make sure they're strong! But if you would like to have the Governor simply enter grandly on foot, that would be fine also.

Kongjee and Patjee

A little more information . . .

Korea Today

Korea has been called the "Land of the Morning Calm." Its history has not been calm, however. Wars have torn it into two parts.

Though North Korea is under communist control, South Korea is free and under its own rule. People are becoming more modern, with increased technology and education. They dress in traditional Korean attire for holidays and other special occasions, but they usually wear modern clothing. South Koreans live mostly in houses or apartments in busy cities, such as Seoul, the capital of South Korea and its largest city.

Some people, however, still live in traditional Korean cottages, made with clay, brick or cement walls with thatched roofs. Floors are warm in Korean homes, the result of a system of heating called ondol. Pipes are buried under the floors and carry heat from the kitchen to the rest of the house. This is especially comfortable for children who keep their mattresses and quilts in closets and roll them out on the floor at night to sleep.

Much rice is eaten by Korean families, along with grilled meats, fish soup, vegetables, and kimchi, a pickled, vegetable dish. This dish is made with cabbage, radishes, garlic, and red peppers. No one would want to eat kimchi without a drink handy—it is quite spicy! Korean children enjoy persimmons that have been threaded onto strings and hung outside to dry and become sweet.

Long ago, only the children of Korean leaders attended school, but that has changed in modern times. In South Korea, children go to primary school for six years, Monday through Friday and a half day on Saturday. Then they may go to middle school for grades seven through nine, but this costs their families money. After middle school, some students go on to high school and some go to special schools to learn useful skills. There are over two hundred colleges in South Korea.

South Korean children ride bicycles and watch television. They play baseball and practice the martial art of taekwondo (tie-kwon-doh). They are respectful of their teachers and other elders. They salute the Korean flag every morning and at the end of every day, because they are very proud of their beautiful, forward-moving country!

Props

- Two hair ribbons (for Father in his first scene)

- A piece of rope (for Doki in her first scene—optional)

- A red ribbon for Kongjee, and one for The Black Ox and all Sparrows

- Two hoes

- A note (in The Black Ox's pocket)

- A basket of apples

- Two tea cups

- Something to represent straw mats with rice—possibly brown paper rolled out with rice glued on, or actual straw mats from an import store or someone's home

- Kongjee's crown

Scenery

Not too much scenery is needed, but you will need to designate several different parts of your acting area to represent different places in which the action takes place. The play can begin center stage, but Kongjee will need an area, perhaps far stage right, to represent the pantry where she falls asleep. She'll need some fabric to represent her bedroll.

The hillside area can be far stage left. You may wish to decorate it with artificial greenery and a few rocks, or it can be left to the imagination of the actors and audience.

Here are a couple of suggestions for the Sparrow scene, with the rice spread out on straw mats. Choose some different area of your classroom or performance area and have the mats pre-set, or have the Sparrows or Villagers quietly roll them out center stage behind Doki and Kongjee as they discuss the May Festival. Then, when the scene is over and Kongjee leaves for the festival, the Sparrows can roll them up and get them out of the way.

Put on your creative directing hat to plan the last two scenes. Could Kongjee walk all the way around the classroom as she recalls the events of the day, ending up back at the center stage area, newly cleared of mats by the Sparrows? Then the Governor enters the scene and she runs stage left to escape him. As the Groomsmen discuss the Governor's loneliness and their hurting feet, the Villagers and the Farmers' Dancers enter, and we play the Festival stage left. (Perhaps the Governor and Groomsmen walk all the way around the classroom to reach the Festival as well.) The final scene, then, takes place center stage, with the trying on of the shoe front and center.

Costumes

As discussed in the Notes to the Teacher/Director, you may wish to costume this play traditionally. Students may wish to check out library books or visit sites on the Internet to get ideas for traditional Korean attire. If this is not within your grasp, you may wish to suggest the flowing lines of Korean clothing by choosing loose-fitting drawstring pants and blouses.

Kongjee and Patjee

Here are some more specific suggestions:

Kongjee should, of course, look shabby and her clothing should be dull in color, and a bit soiled. Maybe she has a simple apron on over her clothing, which could consist of a loose fitting cotton top and skirt or drawstring pants. Kongjee should wear simple, worn-looking shoes. You might want to buy some inexpensive canvas slippers from an Asian market and "weather" them. Her father could look much the same, with a plain outfit of clothes, but perhaps "flip-flop" style sandals. Doki and Patjee should look much grander, in bright colors with ribbons in their hair. They would probably wear skirts or dresses with sashes rather than pants.

The Black Ox should wear, of course, all black! (Make sure he has a pocket for his note.) His horns can be a lot of fun for the class to design and make—are they two pieces of Styrofoam (painted black) attached to a length of black ribbon, which is tied under his chin? Are they construction paper cones, bobby-pinned into his hair? Or can a class member secure a baseball style hat with horns already attached, representing some local sports team?

The Sparrows should match each other as closely as possible—perhaps they could all wear gray sweat clothing. Grey tops and black pants would also be fine. Or maybe they could wear blouses or shirts in a variety of sparrow-like colors, such as gray, brown and tan. If you like, you could cut "wings" out of posterboard, have the class color them to represent feathers, and attach them to the actors' tops with safety pins—but actors' flapping arms will no doubt create the illusion just as well.

The Governor and his Groomsmen should dress the most grandly of all. Dress them in royal blue, red, and gold, with a construction paper or party supply store crown on the Governor. The Villagers can dress in an assortment of loosely belted attire, with those who dance the Farmers' Dance wearing hats with long white ribbons attached. These hats can be made of straw, with the ribbons attached to the brim, or of cone-shaped construction paper with the ribbons seeming to come out of the top. (You may wish to call attention to the Farmers' Dancers by dressing them in solid white.)

(The play begins with KONGJEE speaking to the audience.)

Kongjee Good morning, everyone, and thank you for coming to our play today. My name is Kongjee and I am a Korean girl. Today my life is happy and all is well, but it was not always so. Won't you listen, while I tell you my story?

My mother died when I was young. My father was left alone to raise me.

(Enter FATHER, who is holding up two hair ribbons, not knowing which one to pick, looking frustrated.)

He did the best he could, but, as I grew older, he decided that I needed a mother and he needed a wife. So he married a woman named Doki.

(Enter DOKI, tugging her daughter PATJEE by the hand. She snatches the hair ribbons out of FATHER's hand and ties them into PATJEE's hair.)

She had a daughter of her own. Her name was Patjee. When they moved into our home, the sky became cloudy and cold winds blew.

(KONGJEE enters the scene with FATHER, DOKI, and PATJEE.)

Patjee Oh mother, I hate this ribbon! It doesn't look good with my coloring! Tie it in Kongjee's old hair and get me another ribbon!

Doki Now, Patjee, don't be grumpy. This ribbon looks so beautiful in your hair! And besides *(Aside, to PATJEE)* I have another ribbon for the dirty pigling's hair—a piece of rope!

Kongjee Father? Did you call for me?

Father Yes, my precious Kongjee. I wonder if you would prepare a meal for me.

Kongjee Of course, Father, I would be happy to cook for you.

Multicultural Plays

Kongjee and Patjee

Doki Oh no, she can't cook right now! The floor is filthy and must be swept! The jug is empty and must be filled with water. And we have moved all of our things into Kongjee's room, so she must make herself a bed in the pantry. *(Aside, to PATJEE)* If the mice will scoot over and make room!

Kongjee I'll be happy to sweep and fill the water jug—but must I really give up my room and move to the pantry? It's quite cold and damp there.

Father *(Looking tired)* Yes, Kongjee, Doki and Patjee are . . . our family now . . . We must treat them with respect and welcome them into our home.

Kongjee Yes, Father. I'll go prepare my bed at once.

Father And then you'll make some supper?

Patjee I thought she had to clean the floor and fill the jug with water!

Doki Oh, Patjee, how clever of you to remember! Yes, those are the most important chores and THEN she'll make you a little something to eat, my dear! Surely you're not so hungry that you would have Kongjee cook instead of doing the things that I, her new stepmother, would like her to do?

Father No, I . . . I suppose that is the last thing I want. Kongjee, I think that I am not hungry after all. Please do as your stepmother asks. *(FATHER exits.)*

Doki Now, you dirty little pig. Your easy life is over! Get to work before I get angry!

Kongjee Yes, Onomi.

Doki What? You call me "Onomi," the word for Mother? Patjee is my only daughter! Now get down to the pantry and shoo the mice out of your new bedroom!

(DOKI and PATJEE exit, giggling. KONGJEE crosses to her bedroom area.)

Kongjee If only my real Onomi were here! I miss her so. All I have to remember her by is this piece of red ribbon.

Kongjee and Patjee

(KONGJEE pulls the red ribbon out from under her garments where it has been hidden. Clutching it lovingly, she rolls out a piece of cloth on which to sleep and begins to sing.)

(See music page 47)
ALL OF THE PRETTY DAYS ARE GONE

DAYS OF LOVE WITH MY MOTHER

HOW WILL I BE STRONG? HOW WILL I KEEP A SMILE?

I WILL HOLD A SONG IN MY HEART

I WILL KEEP HER EYES IN MY EYES

MAYBE HER LOVE WILL GIVE ME HOPE.

REMEMBERING HER LOVE WILL MAKE ME SMILE.

(Yawning) Oh my . . . I'll sweep and fill the water jug first thing tomorrow . . .

(KONGJEE pulls a piece of cloth over herself and falls asleep.)

(In a few moments, a cast member makes a crowing rooster noise offstage to indicate that it is now morning. DOKI and PATJEE enter.)

Doki Kongjee! Kongjee! Are you going to sleep all morning! There are chores to do, child, get up!

Kongjee (Hurriedly getting out of bed) Good morning, Doki. Good morning, Patjee. Did you sleep well?

Patjee Not very well. Birds began chirping at my window just as hai, the sun, came up this morning! They disturbed me!

Kongjee Oh! Those are my friends the sparrows. They sing to me every morning to help me wake up.

Patjee They'll be getting a pot of cold water thrown on them if they make that much noise every morning!

Doki (Handing hoes to the girls) All right, you two girls, it's time to clear the fields. Patjee, you take the small, soft little patch of land right outside the kitchen. I'll be able to see you from inside and bring you water if you become hot or tired. Kongjee—you take the hillside.

Multicultural Plays

Kongjee But Stepmother—the hillside is huge and full of rocks and weeds! I shall be old and stooped over before I finish!

Doki Then you had better work fast while you still have your strength! Now off with you! Patjee, please drink a cup of tea with me before you go. You'll need your strength. Kongjee—hurry up, child! You don't want to be old and stooped before the hillside is clear! Come, Patjee, let's go have our tea. *(They exit.)*

Kongjee *(Crossing to the hillside area with her hoe)* Oh my, look at this! The whole hillside is covered with weeds and filled with rocks! How can she expect me to . . . oh well, I guess I'll never finish if I don't start!

(She begins to hoe.)

(Enter BLACK OX. He has a red ribbon tied on one of his horns.)

Black Ox Er . . . excuse me . . . Kongjee? Is that you?

Kongjee *(Looking up from her hoeing)* Yes? Did you speak to me, Ox?

Black Ox Unless you are a mind-reading child! What do they call those—psychics? Or are they "sidekicks"? I get mixed up.

Kongjee What in the world are you doing here? I've never seen a black ox before, only brown!

Black Ox Let's just say that I'm rather special. So are you, and that's why I'm here!

Kongjee I'm confused!

Black Ox You think YOU'RE confused! I'm a black ox, standing in the middle of a field, having a conversation with a girl! I'm really turned around! Oh, wait, I have a note here somewhere. *(BLACK OX pats his pockets and finally finds a tiny scrap of paper.)* Oh yes, now I remember. You have been noticed in heaven, Kongjee, for being so sweet and kind. I have been sent to help you out!

Kongjee In heaven? How is it that you have that red ribbon tied on your horn, Black Ox?

Black Ox Red ribbon? *(Reaching up and feeling it)* Why, I didn't know it was there! How odd! I must've gotten up on the weird side of the field this morning!

Kongjee You're here to help me? How?

Black Ox Child, you insult me! You're supposed to clear this field, right?

Kongjee Yes I am, and it will take forever!

Black Ox Oh no it won't, now that I'm on the job! Stand back, little missy, there may be flying rocks!

(He begins to rush around the hillside area, pantomiming eating weeds and throwing rocks with his mighty horns.)

(KONGJEE claps her hands and laughs out loud as BLACK OX tears around the area.)

Kongjee Look at him go! I never saw an ox move so fast! He must be magic!

Black Ox *(Bowing before her)* Ta da! All finished!

Kongjee Oh my friendly ox, how can I ever thank you?

Black Ox Just be patient and continue to be the kind and loving girl that you are. Oh! I almost forgot! *(He exits briefly and comes back with a basket of apples.)* These are for you!

Kongjee How did you know that I have not had breakfast?

Black Ox Just a hunch.

Kongjee Thank you Black Ox. I will never forget you.

Black Ox And in heaven, you will not be forgotten, little Kongjee. Now good-bye! *(He exits.)*

 Kongjee and Patjee

Kongjee *(Waving)* Good-bye!

(KONGJEE begins to polish an apple on her clothing as she walks back to the house. DOKI and PATJEE meet her, holding their tea cups.)

Doki Kongjee! What are you doing back home?

Patjee Is the whole hillside clear?

Doki Not likely. She's not an old woman yet!

(DOKI and PATJEE laugh.)

Patjee What are you eating? Are those apples?

Kongjee Yes, Doki and Patjee, I brought you some apples for your lunch! See how red and beautiful they are?

Doki Where did you steal these, little piglet?

Kongjee Nowhere, Stepmother. A black ox gave them to me after he finished clearing the hillside for me!

(DOKI and PATJEE look at each other, then back at the audience, then they burst out laughing.)

Patjee What tales she brings home to us! What lies!

Doki A black ox! There is no such thing! All oxen are brown! This proves she's making up stories!

Kongjee Look at the hillside and see for yourself, Stepmother.

(DOKI and PATJEE strain to look out the window and then turn around shocked.)

Patjee It's evil magic, that's what it is!

Doki Yes, some sort of trickery. Some tokgabis no doubt!

Patjee Don't worry, Kongjee, you'll get what you deserve.

Doki Little piglings always end up in the mud!

(DOKI and PATJEE laugh together.)

Kongjee and Patjee

Kongjee Where is my father?

Doki I sent him . . . that is, he went into town to buy a few things at the market. He'll not be back before dark.

Kongjee *(Sadly)* Oh.

Doki And what a shame, he'll miss the festival.

Kongjee Oh! The May festival!

Doki Yes yes, it starts today.

Patjee What on earth will I wear?! I haven't a thing!

Doki Go look in Kongjee's things, darling; maybe she has something you can bear to put on.

Patjee Not likely! *(She exits.)*

Kongjee Oh, Stepmother! I love the May Festival! I didn't realize that today is the first day! I love the Farmers' Dance with the long white ribbons attached to the farmers' hats! I love to watch the acrobats and taste all the lovely food! The governor even comes, did you know that?

Doki Oh yes! And this year it should be even more spectacular than in years past. What a shame you won't be able to attend!

Kongjee Oh Stepmother, surely you'll allow me to go to the May Festival! I've finished clearing the hillside.

Doki Well, Kongjee, I don't want you to think I'm completely without a heart—here is what I'll allow. I've taken the rice from its bundles and spread it out on straw mats behind the house. When you have removed each kernel of rice from its hull, you may join us at the May Festival.

Kongjee But Stepmother! There are bundles and bundles of rice! How can I possibly finish in time?

Doki   Hmmm, I'm sure I don't know! Perhaps another black ox will come along? One with nimble little fingers? Ha ha . . . ha ha ha! *(She exits laughing.)*

(KONGJEE crosses to the area where the straw mats are spread out.)

Kongjee   *(In despair)* How in the world will I ever finish even the tiniest portion of this rice? *(She sighs.)* Oh well—I guess I'll just start and see how far I get.

(Enter SPARROWS, tiptoeing quietly, all wearing a red ribbon somewhere on their costumes.)

First Sparrow   Kongjee?

Second Sparrow   Kongjee! Look up!

Third Sparrow   Your friends the sparrows are here to help you!

Kongjee   My friends . . . what? The sparrows who once sang at my window and brightened my mornings?

First Sparrow   Yes, we used to sing! When someone pure of heart was in your bedroom instead of those two . . .

Second Sparrow   Be kind!

Third Sparrow   How can she be kind?! Those two beasts have ruined everything!

First Sparrow   Remember—she must be patient, and so must we.

Third Sparrow   We're here to help hull the rice, Kongjee!

Second Sparrow   You've never seen anybody hull rice like sparrows can!

Kongjee   There is good magic in the world after all!

First Sparrow   You just wait, Kongjee! You haven't seen anything yet!

Kongjee and Patjee

(The SPARROWS pantomime hulling rice and blowing away the husks while they sing.)

(See music page 48) IT'S MAY! IT'S MAY! COME ON EVERYONE, LET'S PLAY!

NO ONE MAY STAY AT HOME, OPEN DOORS, FREE TO ROAM.

IT'S MAY! IT'S MAY! NO MORE CHORES TO DO TODAY!

KONGJEE CHANGE YOUR DUSTY DRESS, FIX YOUR HAIR, LOOK YOUR BEST!

WE SING! WE SING! OF JOY THE SPRINGTIME BRINGS!

LOTS OF FUN WAITS JUST FOR YOU

(first sparrow) AND FOR ME!

(second sparrow) AND ME TOO!

WE SING! WE SING! AND WE FLUTTER JOYOUS WINGS.

WE'RE YOUR FRIENDS 'CAUSE YOU'RE SO NICE, NOW JUST LOOK AT THE RICE!

Kongjee IT'S DONE!

Sparrows IT'S DONE! NOW WE CAN ENJOY THE SUN!

Kongjee Oh, I don't know what to say! How did I earn such loyal friends?

First Sparrow You mean you don't know?

Second Sparrow She really doesn't.

Third Sparrow You're good and kind and patient. Now hurry—the Festival is starting!

Kongjee Shouldn't I change my clothes?

First Sparrow No, don't take time! You'll be late!

Kongjee Goodbye, little sparrows! I'll never forget you!

All Sparrows Goodbye, Kongjee! Have a good time! Bye!

(KONGJEE walks along, on her way to the Festival.)

Multicultural Plays

Kongjee and Patjee

Kongjee Oh, what an odd day! It seemed so sad at first, with Doki and Patjee being disagreeable, but then things changed so much! First the black ox helped me clear the hillside, and then my friends the sparrows hulled the rice! And they didn't even eat any of it! *(She stumbles.)* Ouch, a pebble in my shoe! I must take it out or I will never be able to walk all the way to the Festival. *(She removes her shoe.)* Why . . . what's that I hear?

(Enter the GOVERNOR and his GROOMSMEN.)

Governor What a lovely day for the Festival! I can't wait to arrive! I only wish I was a married gentleman, that I might share the joy of the day with my wife.

(KONGJEE sees the GOVERNOR coming and is alarmed.)

Kongjee The governor! I can't let him see me in such dirty work clothes! I must run away.

Governor *(Seeing KONGJEE)* Wait! Young lady! Don't be afraid!

Kongjee Forgive me, sir—I am not worthy to see such a man as you! *(She exits, running and leaving her shoe behind.)*

Governor Young lady, wait! Don't go! *(He sees her shoe.)* What's this? Fetch me that shoe!

(One of the GROOMSMEN picks up the shoe and hands it to the GOVERNOR.)

Governor She was not only beautiful, but so humble, saying she was not worthy to see me! I must meet her. Let's pursue her! I must meet the girl who lost this slipper!

First Groomsman Let's hope she runs slowly!

Second Groomsman Yes! The lonelier he gets—the more my feet hurt!

(ALL exit.)

(KONGJEE and other PEOPLE OF THE VILLAGE are eating pieces of fruit and watching the Farmers' Dance. DOKI AND PATJEE are there, but not sitting near KONGJEE, and have not seen her. KONGJEE is having a wonderful time. The dance ends and everyone applauds. The GOVERNOR and his GROOMSMEN approach the crowd.)

Kongjee and Patjee

First Groomsman Attention, everyone! On behalf of the Governor, I ask that you pay attention to what I say!

Kongjee Oh no! The Governor!

Second Groomsman A few miles down the road, the Governor encountered a young woman who left behind this shoe!

Governor I demand to find its owner! Come, ladies! Try it on!

Doki *(Coming forward, seeing the shoe)* Oh, sir! Was there trouble? Do you seek to arrest the owner of the shoe on some charge? If so, will you follow me to my home that I may surrender my stepdaughter Kongjee. I'm certain I've seen that very shoe on her foot!

Governor Quite the contrary! I thought the owner of this shoe was the most beautiful creature in the world, with a humble heart and full of goodness.

Doki Allow me to introduce my daughter Patjee. *(She shoves PATJEE forward.)* Try on the shoe, quickly!

Patjee Oh yes, I recognize this slipper! Let me just . . . *(Trying to force her foot in)* . . . I'm sure it will fit in a moment . . .

Governor Good heavens, you'll rip it at the seams. Wait! There! *(He sees KONGJEE.)* There is the young woman!

Doki Kongjee? What are you doing here? I told you to . . .

Governor Silence, madam. I wish for her to try on this shoe.

Doki That is just what I wish. This is my lovely stepdaughter Kongjee, whom I have raised since . . . since yesterday.

Governor *(To KONGJEE)* Were you not the young woman on the path?

Kongjee *(Shyly coming forward)* Yes.

Governor Why did you run away?

Kongjee I am just a poor farm girl, Sir. I didn't want you to look upon my dusty clothes and hands dirty from working in the field.

Multicultural Plays

Governor Try on this slipper, please.

(She tries on the slipper, which fits. The crowd cheers. FATHER enters.)

Father Kongjee! What is going on? Doki, why didn't you tell me you were coming to the May Festival!

Doki Oh, it must have slipped my mind.

Governor Sir, may I have the honor of your daughter's hand in marriage?

Father Governor, what joy you bring to us this day! Is this what you would like, Kongjee?

Kongjee Father, Governor, I don't think I'm worthy of such a proposal.

(THE SPARROWS and BLACK OX enter, all still wearing their red ribbons.)

Black Ox *(Pointing upward)* Oh, Kongjee. Someone up there thinks you are!

Father Marry the Governor, my precious daughter. He will be able to give you a better life than I have.

Kongjee Yes Governor, of course I would be honored. As long as my family may come with us to the palace.

Governor Of course they may. Perhaps we can teach your stepmother some things about being good hearted!

First Groomsman I'm sure that can be arranged!

Doki *(Bowing)* I am your humble servant.

(The GOVERNOR and KONGJEE hold hands and the SPARROWS set a crown on KONGJEE's head, while the whole cast says:)

Cast And they all lived happily ever after! *(Waving)* Goodbye! Thank you for coming!

Mother In My Heart

Words by Judy Truesdell Mecca

Music by Jenifer Truesdell Christman

Multicultural Plays

Kongjee and Patjee

The Sparrow Song

Words by Judy Truesdell Mecca

Music by Jenifer Truesdell Christman

Cora, Who Will Be A Poet
A Play Set in Mexico

Multicultural Plays

Cora, Who Will Be A Poet

CAST

Cora

Paloma,
Cora's sister

Mamá

Papá

Grandmother

Tía Maria,
Cora's aunt

Tony,
Cora's brother

Arturo,
Cora's brother

Chorus

Cora, Who Will Be A Poet

Notes to the Teacher/Director

Mexico, our vibrant and colorful neighbor to the south, is a land of many extremes. Large, teeming cities, such as Mexico City, have many high-rise office buildings, apartment houses, and places to shop and dine out. Families who live here enjoy conveniences such as dishwashers and washing machines, and some have hired help to do the cooking and cleaning.

Most Mexicans, however, are not so well off. About one-fourth of all Mexicans live in more rural areas, some in poverty, some on large farms, or ranchos. Many of the farm houses are modest, with few rooms. Until recent years, many of the homes did not have even electricity or running water; however, the Mexican government has made great strides in bringing these conveniences to all homes. Corn continues to be the main crop of Mexico, as it has been since ancient times. Other crops include beans, squash, peppers, cucumbers, and tomatoes when the growing season has been rainy.

The family is a vital part of life in Mexico. Many members of the same family live together in one house—grandmothers and grandfathers, aunts (or tías) and uncles, mothers and fathers, and their children. Educational opportunities are improving every year for Mexican children. Mandatory public education exists through ninth grade; nevertheless, some children still drop out long before that time to work on their families' farms.

Our play, *Cora, Who Will Be a Poet*, incorporates several elements of modern Mexico. The main characters live together on a farm, one that is doing well. This is good news—but not so good for Cora, the young woman who enjoys writing poetry and getting an education at the local school. When her parents ask her to stay home to care for her younger brothers, freeing the parents to work the farm, she is sad. She agrees readily, however, not only because she feels she must put the needs of the family first, but also because her father has asked this of her. In Mexico, the father is very much the head of the household and must be obeyed. However, when she reads a poem aloud that she has written to her grandfather, her talent is recognized by her family and she is granted permission to continue with her education.

Another of Mexico's traditional elements included in *Cora, Who Will Be a Poet*, is that of El Diá De Los Muertos—the Day of the Dead celebration. On November 2, Mexicans celebrate their departed loved ones in a festival. They decorate their homes and streets with construction paper skeletons and make candies in the shape of skulls. They line the streets with marigolds, a flower thought to lead the dead back to their loved ones. The children decorate shoe boxes to

Cora, Who Will Be A Poet

look like skulls and go door to door, asking, "Will you give some candy for the skull?" calling to mind American children's Halloween trick-or-treating. The Day of the Dead celebration is a happy, joyous event, celebrating and remembering loved ones who are no longer alive. It culminates in a picnic at the gravesites of the ones being honored, in which the departed's favorite foods and drinks are taken and laid graveside.

In addition to the speaking roles in our play, other young actors may be incorporated as the Chorus. This group sings as it makes the scene change from the farmhouse to the cemetery. The actors can then remain in the cemetery scene in the background if you like, and then lead the Day of the Dead parade around the classroom, hoisting paper skeletons, wearing skull make-up, and singing. It might be fun to incorporate maracas or other musical instruments if someone knows how to play!

Your cast can personalize the play for added enjoyment. Cora has written two poems, which she reads in the play. You may of course use the ones included, or it might be fun to have your class write their own poems—one about a donkey and one dedicated to Cora's grandfather—and have the class vote on ones to use instead of the printed poetry. In addition, when they visit their grandfather's grave, Papá takes along Grandfather's favorite brand of soda. Your class can vote on the brand name to insert in the blank—and they may wish to add a line from a current commercial about that soft drink.

COMMON SPANISH EXPRESSIONS

Spanish is the native language of Mexico, where our play takes place. Following are some common Spanish words and phrases, and how to pronounce them.

Buenos días.	(BWAY nos DEE ahs) Good morning.
¿Cómo está usted?	(KOH moh es TAH oo STEDH) How are you?
hombre	(ohm BRAY) man
mujer	(moo HEHR) woman
sí	(see) yes
no	(noh) no
por favor	(por fah VOR) please
Gracias	(GRAH see ahs) Thank you.
De nada	(day NAH dah) You're welcome.
Hasta Luego	(AHS tah loo AY goh) So long.
Lo siento	(loh see EN toh) I'm sorry.
¡Qué bueno!	(kay BWAY no) Great!

Cora, Who Will Be A Poet

A recipe . . .

PAN DE MUERTO—BREAD OF THE DEAD

In the play, Mamá is busily making her special recipe for Bread of the Dead to take to the cemetery. Perhaps your cast would like to make this special bread themselves! Please make sure an adult helps out!

What you'll need:

- ¼ cup milk
- ¼ cup sugar, plus
- 2 teaspoons sugar, separated
- ¼ cup (half a stick) margarine or butter
- ½ teaspoon salt
- 1 package active dry yeast
- ¼ cup hot water (from the tap)
- 2 eggs
- 3 cups all-purpose flour, not sifted
- ½ teaspoon anise seed
- ¼ teaspoon ground cinnamon
- 1 cup flour (to flour the countertop)

How to make it:

Put milk in a saucepan and bring to a boil on the stove. Remove it from heat. Stir in ¼ cup sugar, all butter, and salt.

In a large bowl, mix yeast with hot water until it is dissolved. Let it stand five minutes, then add the milk mixture.

Separate the yolk and white of one egg. Add the yolk to the yeast mixture, but save the white for the glaze. Add another whole egg to the mixture.

Add the flour to the yeast and eggs. Blend well until it forms a dough ball.

Put flour on a countertop or pastry board and place the dough on it. Knead it with your hands until it is smooth. Then return it to a large bowl and cover with a dish towel. Put it in a warm place and let it rise for one and one-half hours.

Preheat the oven to 350 degrees and grease a baking sheet.

Knead dough again on the floured countertop. Divide the dough into fourths and set one piece aside. Now make "ropes" out of the three remaining pieces and, on a greased baking sheet, "braid" them together and pinch together the ends. Divide the remaining bit of dough in half and make it form two "bone" shapes. Lay them across the braided loaf.

Cover bread with a dish towel and let it rise for 30 minutes. During this time, mix anise seed, cinnamon, and the two teaspoons of sugar together. Beat egg white lightly.

After 30 minutes, brush the top of the bread with egg white and sprinkle with the sugar mixture—except on the crossbones!

Bake at 350 degrees for 35 minutes.

Multicultural Plays

Cora, Who Will Be A Poet

Props

- Kitchen items for making breakfast, including:
  - Coffee pot and coffee cups
  - Plates
  - Silverware
  - Tortillas
  - A bowl of beans
- A broken hoe
- Scissors and white paper (for making skeletons)
- Cora's journal and a pencil
- A ball for Arturo and Tony
- A hairbrush and ribbon
- Cora and Paloma's school books
- A sheet of paper to represent Cora's poem about the donkey
- The items for the picnic, including:
  - Blankets
  - A can of soft drink
  - Tortillas
  - Corn
  - Marigolds
  - The picture Tony has drawn of himself and Arturo
  - The Bread of the Dead, a knife to cut it and some paper plates on which to serve it
- Cora's poem to her grandfather
- Decorations and masks for the Chorus and the audience. Gather several life-sized skeletons made of paper or white plastic, candy skulls, little plastic skeletons or costume jewelry, and shoe boxes decorated as skulls.

Scenery

Only two scenes are needed for the play. The first, in the farmhouse, can be easily represented with a table and two chairs, and perhaps some desks pushed together and covered with a cloth to represent the area where the women are cooking. You will probably wish to put the table and chairs in the front (downstage) so that the important action will receive most attention.

The cemetery is the setting for the other scene and what fun your class can have creating tombstones and decorating for the Day of the Dead! The best way to make tombstones is to use Styrofoam that you have painted gray. It will provide the thickness of a tombstone, but will be light enough for your young chorus members to move around. Your students will probably have many ideas for the inscriptions, which they can inscribe on the tombstones with paint or markers. Use as many tombstones as space allows—the only one you really must have is Grandfather's. You may wish to add some greenery, real or construction paper, to your cemetery area. You can string marigolds into garlands and then "carpet" the grave areas during this festival. Real marigolds would be wonderful if you can find them—if not, you might experiment with gold-colored tissue paper blossoms. Candles are sometimes lit in the cemetery as well, the idea being that the dead can smell the smoke from the fire and will be led to the party! You may wish to omit the candles from your scenery, however, to ensure the safety of your young cast.

Costumes

Clothing in Mexico today is a rich combination of traditional Mexican attire and more modern clothing. The adult women in the play should probably be clad in loose, comfortable house dresses, perhaps with aprons. (You'll want to experiment with some make-up for Grandmother—perhaps some baby powder in her hair, and some glasses on the end of her nose.) When they go to the cemetery, however, you might have some of the women wear a rebozo, a type of shawl. Papá can wear overalls over a comfortable workshirt, or he might be dressed in loose white cotton trousers, as is the custom in some areas of Mexico. (White is worn to keep cool while working in the fields.) Don't forget to put a bandanna in Papa's shirt pocket so he can use it to wipe away his tears when Cora reads her poem.

Cora, Who Will Be A Poet

Nearly all school children in Mexico dress in uniforms, so Cora and Paloma should wear dark skirts and white blouses, and perhaps dark sweaters. Because they won't have much time to change before the cemetery scene, you may wish to give them different, brightly colored sweaters or shawls for that scene.

The boys will probably be fine in jeans and plaid shirts or workshirts.

You can add color and fun to the play by dressing some of your Chorus members in traditional attire. One or two large hats called sombreros, gaily colored wool blankets tossed over a shoulder, full skirts—all can be interspersed with regular jeans and skirts and blouses. Many of your cast members should already have their faces made up to look like skulls, with dark circles around their eyes, noses, and mouths, and the rest of their faces painted white. You can purchase make-up at a party supply store. Some may wish to wrap hoods around their heads. The cast members portraying the family members will not have time to apply make-up to their faces before the final parade, but some of them might wish to put on skeleton masks that they have made in advance.

Cora, Who Will Be A Poet

(As the play begins, we see a Mexican family in their farmhouse kitchen. GRANDMOTHER, MAMÁ, and TÍA MARIA are making a breakfast of corn tortillas, beans, and coffee. PAPÁ is seated at the table, drinking his first cup of coffee, trying to repair a hoe that has broken. Two young boys, TONY and ARTURO are playing with a ball. PALOMA, their sister, is cutting the skeleton shapes out of white paper, and CORA, their other sister, is at the table with PAPÁ, writing in a book of some kind. She shields her work with her hand so that her PAPÁ cannot see it.)

Mamá   Paloma, stop working on those skeletons and eat your breakfast. You'll be late for school.

Paloma   Oh, Mamá, just one more snip! There! *(She holds up a paper skeleton.)* What do you think?

Tony   *(Looking up)* I think it looks just like you!

Arturo   No, Tony—the skeleton is much prettier than Paloma!

Paloma   Be quiet, both of you little pests. Mamá, I'm so excited about the Day of the Dead celebration! Roberto at school says that he will bring candy skulls for all of the class!

Papá   That will be a large number of skulls! How many are in your class now?

Paloma   About sixty. His father and mother make the candy skulls somehow, in their kitchen.

Mamá   Maybe I will call Señora Flores and ask her for the recipe.

Grandmother   Better not, my dear! She may ask you for your recipe for Bread of the Dead in return!

Papá   No one can ever know that recipe! Your Pan de Muerto is the best in town.

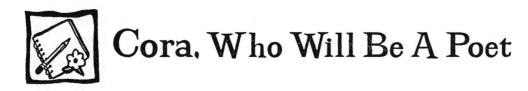

Cora, Who Will Be A Poet

Mamá You are all flattering me so I'll be sure to make it again this year! Don't worry! I'll be starting to bake it this very morning.

Tía Maria Come here, Paloma, let me brush your hair so you'll look pretty for school.

(PALOMA crosses to her aunt, who brushes her hair, perhaps styling it with a ribbon.)

Tía Maria *(As she works)* Cora? Would you like for me to brush your hair, my little dove?

Cora *(Looking up for the first time)* I am sorry, Tía Maria, what did you say?

Papá She asked you if you would like her to fix your hair, for school.

Cora Oh, no, thank you Tía. I'd like to keep writing.

Paloma Oh, Cora, please don't keep it a secret! Please read aloud some of your . . .

Cora *(Interrupting)* Paloma! You promised not to tell!

Grandmother Tell what, little ones? Your mother never kept any secrets from me!

Mamá That is what you think, my dear mother.

Grandmother What shocking news for an old lady to hear!

Mamá *(To her daughter)* Cora, dear, what secret do you keep?

Paloma It is a wonderful secret, Mamá! Cora is so good at . . .

Cora, Who Will Be A Poet

Cora *(Interrupting again)* Paloma is teasing me. There is no secret. Now, I think I must get started for school!

Papá Cora . . . wait a moment.

Cora Yes, Papá?

Papá I need to talk to you about something. Something I do not want to say . . .

Cora Have I done something wrong, Papá? I know I haven't done as well in my history class as I wanted to, but I'll study harder!

Papá No, no, you're a wonderful student and we are very proud. But your mother and I feel . . .

Mamá *(Coming over to the table to help out her husband)* Cora, you know that our rancho has been blessed with a lot of rain this year.

Arturo The corn is taller than I am!

Tony Everything is taller than you are!

(They scuffle.)

Mamá Boys . . .

Papá The corn is very tall and we even have cucumbers and tomatoes for the first time in many years. There is a lot of work to be done . . .

Mamá What your father is trying to say, girls, is that we need you to take some time off from school to help mind your little brothers so we may work on the farm.

Cora, Who Will Be A Poet

Paloma Yippee! Freedom!

Cora What? Time off from school?! But, Papá . . .

Papá It won't be forever, Cora my dear. Just until winter when everything is harvested and sold at market!

Paloma *(Realizing what this means for her sister)* Oh, but Papá, Cora is such a wonderful student. She needs to be in school! I can watch these two pests!

Cora Paloma, it's all right. If Mamá and Papá need me at home, I'll stay here.

Papá Go on to school today, girls. See if the teachers will lend you some books so that you won't get too far behind.

Cora Yes, Papá.

Papá Girls, I am so sorry. It really will not be forever, I promise!

(The girls gather up their few books and pencils and exit.)

Paloma Goodbye, everyone!

Cora (Sadly) Goodbye . . .

(As PALOMA and CORA exit the kitchen and begin walking to school, the rest of the family strikes the kitchen scene and exits.)

Paloma Cora, you make me so angry!

Cora Why in the world do I make you angry, Paloma?

Cora, Who Will Be A Poet

Paloma Because of your silly secret! If Mamá and Papá knew what a wonderful writer you are, and knew about your lovely poetry, they would surely let you stay in school.

Cora My poems are just for myself, Paloma! I don't want to share them.

Paloma You share them with me, sometimes! Read one now, as we walk. Read the one about the donkey!

Cora *(Finding a piece of paper)* Oh, all right. *(reading)*
My little donkey with the sad brown eyes
Walks along slowly, never cries
Nothing too heavy to carry along
His heart is sad but his back is strong
When will he reach the market place
And see the smile on the little boy's face?
My little donkey with the sad brown eyes
Walks very slowly, but he never cries.

(Paloma seems to sniffle.)

Paloma, are you crying? You've heard that poem a hundred times!

Paloma No, I'm just teasing. But it could make me cry! I can see that little sad donkey! In my mind, I see him clearly! In fact . . . I just realized something! You are like that little donkey, Cora!

Cora *(Sarcastically)* Paloma, thank you so much for that compliment! I didn't know you thought I was as beautiful as a donkey!

Paloma I just mean that you are sad. And carrying a heavy load. You should be free to soar and fly!

Multicultural Plays

Cora, Who Will Be A Poet

Cora A flying donkey! Quite a picture, Paloma!

(They laugh together.)

Paloma We had better hurry, or we'll be late! Come on, Cora, I'll race you!

Cora Last one there has to kiss Roberto Flores!

Paloma Oh no! Not that!

(As the girls exit, racing, the CHORUS enters and begins setting up the cemetery for the Day of the Dead picnic. As they set the stage, they sing:)

(See music page 68) ¡HOLA! WELCOME THE DAY OF THE DEAD
IT'S TIME FOR A FESTIVAL, GET OUT OF YOUR BED!
JOIN US TO SING, AND EAT SPECIAL BREAD
SKELETONS DANCE—IT'S THE DAY OF THE DEAD!

DON'T BE AFRAID, YOU SHOULD LAUGH AND SING
LOOK IN MY BASKET! WHAT DID YOU BRING?
JOIN THE FIESTA, ENJOY CANDY TREATS
THAT SKELETON HEAD MAY BE GOOD TO EAT!

¡HOLA! WELCOME THE DAY OF THE DEAD
IT'S TIME FOR A FESTIVAL, GET OUT OF YOUR BED!
JOIN US TO SING, AND EAT SPECIAL BREAD
SKELETONS DANCE—IT'S THE DAY OF THE DEAD!

(Following the song, CHORUS members may exit or divide into small groups around the cemetery and pantomime talking and unpacking picnics. Enter MAMÁ, PAPÁ, GRANDMOTHER, TÍA MARIA, ARTURO, TONY, PALOMA and CORA, carrying picnic baskets and blankets on which to sit.)

Tía Maria *(Spotting Grandfather's grave)* Here is his grave! Over here!

Cora, Who Will Be A Poet

(The rest of the family joins her and starts spreading out blankets and setting up for a picnic.)

Grandmother *(To the headstone)* Ah, my dear. It seems like only yesterday you were sharing a blanket with me! How I miss you.

Mamá We all miss him, Mother . . . and that's why we're here. To show our love for my father and celebrate his life.

Papá That's right—look, I brought his favorite brand of soda: _____ ! *(Insert favorite brand of soda here.)*

Tía Maria I'm sure he's happy to see that! I brought something too—a stack of tortillas and some corn from the rancho! *(She places it on his grave.)*

Mamá How happy that will make him!

Grandmother He loved the farm as much as we all do.

Tony I brought something for Grandfather! Look, Grandmother—a picture I drew! A picture of me and Arturo! *(He places the picture on the grave.)*

Grandmother How lovely!

Arturo I'm the handsome one . . .

Papá His soul is among us, I feel sure.

Mamá I know it is. Here, I will slice up the Bread of the Dead. Does everyone want a piece?

(All ad-lib "yes," "of course," and MAMÁ serves it as she continues speaking.)

Multicultural Plays

Cora, Who Will Be A Poet

Mamá   Paloma? Cora? Did you bring a present for your grandfather?

Paloma   I did, Mamá. I brought him these marigolds.

Mamá   Ah, what beautiful flowers!

Grandmother   They will lead him to us for sure.

Mamá   And what about you, Cora? A present for my father on the Day of the Dead?

Cora   *(Sighing, seeming to gather strength)* Yes, Mamá. I have something for Grandfather.

Paloma   Go ahead, Cora, read it!

Cora   I wrote a poem for my Grandfather.

Tía Maria   A poem?

Papá   I did not know you had this talent!

Paloma   That's what I've been trying to tell you! Cora writes beautiful, lovely poetry! She has been writing for a long time! She has a book full of it! She's . . .

Cora   Paloma, don't embarrass me. Just let me read this poem for my grandfather.

Grandmother   Cora, I would be most honored to hear it.

Cora, Who Will Be A Poet

Cora *(Reading)*
A Poem for My Grandfather

I wish I could see you with my eyes
But I will see you better with my heart.
I wish you could feel the sun today, shining on my face
But I will remember other sunny days we shared.
I wish we could feel rain together, when it falls
So I'll pretend to share the fresh feeling with you.
I wish so much that I could hold your hand
But always know, you hold my heart.

(MAMÁ and TÍA MARIA rush to hug CORA. PALOMA and the boys clap their hands, and PAPÁ gets out a bandanna and wipes his eyes.)

Grandmother   Cora, what an honor! What a beautiful poem!

Mamá   I never would have guessed.

Paloma   Mamá, Papá, listen to me. We had a lesson in school today about a Mexican poet named Juana Inez de la Cruz. She lived over 300 years ago, in a time when women were not allowed to do the things we can do today. She became a nun and even the church did not want her to write her poems and plays. Our teacher told us that, as the story goes, she had her pen and paper taken from her and so she wrote on the walls of her room with her own blood.

(Crossing to her sister and putting her arm around her)

Cora doesn't live in that time. She lives in a day when women and men can express themselves, with words or paint or clay. Lucky Cora! Look how good she already is—how good will she come to be if she stays in school! Please don't make her stay home.

Multicultural Plays

Cora, Who Will Be A Poet

(A pause, as CORA and PALOMA look expectantly at PAPÁ.)

Tía Maria   I can work part of the time in the fields and the rest of the day with the boys.

Grandmother   And I don't believe that I'm too old to play ball with two youngsters!

Papá   Mamá, I think I have decided . . . yes. I must change my mind.

Mamá   Cora . . . I think Papá is right. We'll work out something for your brothers. Your place is in school.

(All shout and hug and act happy at this news.)

Papá   And you, Paloma. You spoke so well on behalf of your sister. You have a gift of words yourself! You must stay in school also!

Paloma   Wait! Wait, Papá, I'll be happy to stay home!

Mamá   No, it's settled. Both of my girls will go back to school and use their minds in the way God planned for them.

Paloma   *(Under her breath, to CORA)* That'll teach me to speak up!

Cora   My sister! How can I thank you?

Paloma   I'm sure I'll think of something!

(They hug.)

Tía Maria   Now! Let's put on our masks and make-up! It's time for the Day of the Dead Festival!

Cora, Who Will Be A Poet

(The whole CAST joins the family, wearing skeleton make-up, carrying paper skeletons and shoe boxes decorated as skulls. The audience is included in the fun, as skeletons and candy are handed out, and the audience members are invited to join in the march. Then, CAST and audience march around the room, singing once more:)

All ¡HOLA! WELCOME THE DAY OF THE DEAD
IT'S TIME FOR A FESTIVAL, GET OUT OF YOUR BED!
JOIN US TO SING, AND EAT SPECIAL BREAD
SKELETONS DANCE—IT'S THE DAY OF THE DEAD!

DON'T BE AFRAID, YOU SHOULD LAUGH AND SING
LOOK IN MY BASKET! WHAT DID YOU BRING?
JOIN THE FIESTA, ENJOY CANDY TREATS
THAT SKELETON HEAD MAY BE GOOD TO EAT!

¡HOLA! WELCOME THE DAY OF THE DEAD
IT'S TIME FOR A FESTIVAL, GET OUT OF YOUR BED!
JOIN US TO SING, AND EAT SPECIAL BREAD
SKELETONS DANCE—IT'S THE DAY OF THE DEAD!

(Waving) Adiós! Thank you for coming!

Cora, Who Will Be A Poet

Day Of The Dead

Words by Judy Truesdell Mecca

Music by Woody Christman

Ho - la! Wel - come the day of the dead. It's time for a fes - ti - val get out of your bed.

Join us to sing and eat spe - cial bread. Skel - e - tons dance it's the day of the dead.

Don't be af - fraid you should laugh and sing. Look in my bas - ket what did you bring?

Join the fi - e - sta en - joy can - dy treats that skel - e - ton head may be good to eat.

Ho - la! Wel - come the day of the dead. It's time for a fes - ti - val get out of your bed.

Join us to sing and eat spe - cial bread. Skel - e - tons dance it's the day of the dead.

© 1999 by Incentive Publications, Inc.
Nashville, TN

JUAN BOBO AND THE SUNDAY PIG
(Based on Puerto Rican Folklore)

JUAN BOBO AND THE SUNDAY PIG

Cast

✦✦✦✦✦✦✦✦✦✦✦✦

JUANITA
✦
MARTINA
✦
FATHER FERNANDO
✦
SANTIAGO,
Juanita's husband
✦
ROSITA,
Juan Bobo's mother
✦
JUAN BOBO
✦
PIG
✦
CHORUS

JUAN BOBO AND THE SUNDAY PIG

Notes to the Teacher/Director

In many countries and cultures, stories are shared about a foolish character who cannot seem to get anything right. In England he is called "Jack," as well as in some American stories such as *Jack and the Beanstalk*. Costa Rican children hear tales of the foolish "Cricket the Bobo," but in Puerto Rico the simpleton is "Juan Bobo." He is good-hearted, he doesn't mean to mess everything up—but he always does.

Storytelling has played an important role in the culture of the people of the island of Puerto Rico from the time of the native Taino Indians. The Tainos were conquered by the Spanish Conquistadors, who began to import slaves from Africa to work their sugar crops. Puerto Rican folklore, then, is a colorful combination of the Indian, Spanish, and African people who have populated the island for centuries.

Juan Bobo and the Sunday Pig is a dramatization of a Puerto Rican story that has been told for generations. Many versions of the tale exist, but in every one, foolish Juan Bobo decides that the family puerquito, or pig, must be dressed in the best dress of Juan's mother and be allowed to attend Mass.

Opportunities to expand the cast include the song at the end, when as many people as you like may join voices to sing about the silly Juan Bobo, or you can add villagers, heading into church on Sunday morning while Martina and Juanita await their friend on the church steps. (For our purposes, Juan Bobo's mother is called "Rosita," although she is simply referred to as "Juan Bobo's mother" in the folktale.)

This play uses the dramatic convention of scenes that act as "flashbacks." That is, the ladies and Santiago are standing on the church steps awaiting Rosita's arrival, and fearing the worst about what Juan Bobo might have done. While they wait, they remember another time, the day when Juan Bobo dressed up the pig. As they reminisce, we see scenes in a different part of the acting area, depicting Juan Bobo, his mother, and the pig. During these scenes, you will probably wish for Juanita, Martina, and Santiago to simply freeze and await their next scene. They may, if you prefer, simply turn and watch the scenes or exit the acting area and return for each scene. (This may be a lot of entering and exiting—probably having them freeze will be the

JUAN BOBO AND THE SUNDAY PIG

smoothest transition.) Then, when Rosita rushes up to join them, present day action begins and she is really there with her friends. This can be made clear by the addition of a shawl, hat or other costume item to make her look different than she has in the previous remembered scenes.

As Spanish is the native language of Puerto Rico, some Spanish words have been included for added color and fun. Make sure your students know and understand the following words:

puerquito	**pig**
la iglesia	**church**
bueno	**good**
buenos días	**good morning**
aretes	**earrings**
collares	**necklace**
brazalete	**bracelet**
besito	**kiss (little)**
sí	**yes**
Mamacita	**affectionate term for "Mother"**

When Rosita describes her best dress to Juan Bobo, she says "My very best dress is _____. I save it for the most special occasions!" Fill in the blank with the color you choose for Rosita's best dress. Fill in the same color later when Juan Bobo is looking for the dress and says "Now let me see, which one did my mother say was her best dress? Oh yes, I remember! She said it was the _____ one!" (A light color will be best so that the "mud" will show up!)

The actor or actress who portrays the Pig will have an opportunity to show a wide range of emotions using only his or her face! Though Pig has only one line, there is no doubt what is going on in his or her head while being dressed in a dress and mantilla! Encourage your actor or actress to be very expressive. This is one instance in which subtlety can be left behind.

For suggestions as to how to "muddy" Pig, see Costumes.

JUAN BOBO AND THE SUNDAY PIG

A little more information . . .

Puerto Rico Today

"Ko-kee! Ko-kee!" calls the coquí, a miniature tan-colored tree frog that grows to a length of only one inch. It is one of the many wonders that can be found on the island of Puerto Rico. There are also snakes, iguanas, beautiful parrots, pelicans, leatherback turtles, and interesting birds called "blue footed boobies." These birds got their names by being so easy to catch that sailors thought they were not smart. The word "boobies" comes from the Spanish word for "dumb" or "stupid"—bobo!

Puerto Rico is a lush tropical island, which is actually part of the West Indies. Seventy-five percent of the island has hills or mountains and it has 311 miles of coastline. The weather is wet and warm, with temperatures above 70 degrees Fahrenheit all year, and lots of rain.

For many years, Puerto Ricans made a living by raising sugarcane, tobacco, coffee beans, and ginger. But, during the mid-1900s, Governor Luis Munoz Marin started "Operation Bootstrap," a program for bringing new industry and businesses to the island. It offered good tax advantages to companies willing to have their head-quarters on Puerto Rico. Factories that make everything from clothing and shoes to television sets and cameras were built. Medicine has become Puerto Rico's leading product. The tourist industry has also increased, and, as a result, many Puerto Ricans work in restaurants, hotels, and travel agencies. Though some Puerto Ricans still farm or fish for a living, two out of every three Puerto Rican citizens live in large cities.

There is a wide variety of things to see and enjoy about life on this island. A music festival called the Casals Festival is held each year. It is named after Pablo Casals, a cello player, who lived in Puerto Rico. The Festival of San Juan, which includes dances, music, and carnivals, is held each June 24.

The city of San Juan is Puerto Rico's capital, but another interesting city is Arecibo, on the northern coast. Though it dates back to 1556, today it is home to something quite modern—the world's largest radio telescope! The dish of this giant is 1,000 feet across. This telescope was responsible for finding the first planets outside of our own solar system, and continuously monitors the heavens for any signs of extra-terrestrial life. You may have seen this telescope featured in the movie *Contact*.

At this time, Puerto Rico is a commonwealth of the United States. That is, it governs itself, but also belongs to the United States. As a result, it receives certain benefits, such as economic help and the aid of the U.S. military. A recent vote in the United States House of Representatives has allowed Puerto Rico to decide its destiny—should it remain a Commonwealth or become the fifty-first state of the United States of America? Or should it be completely independent? Perhaps these questions will be answered by the time you read this play. In any event, in the true spirit of America, the Puerto Rican people will be allowed to choose their own future.

JUAN BOBO AND THE SUNDAY PIG

Props

- Hand props for the folk at church, such as Bibles, handkerchiefs, purses

- Pig's food trough

- Pig's water bowl

- A black purse

- The accessories for the Pig, including:
    - A dress large enough to fit over Pig's costume
    - Earrings
    - Bracelets
    - Facial powder and puff
    - A mantilla, or lacy scarf

Scenery

Very little scenery is needed. You may wish to suggest the doorway to the church by drawing a cross and a door on the chalkboard, or make a cardboard or foam board likeness and paint it.

You may wish to represent Juan Bobo and Rosita's house by having a table and chairs, perhaps with a bowl of fruit, but it is never specifically mentioned. Rosita's purse, facial powder and mantilla must be produced from somewhere—perhaps several classroom chairs are pushed together to represent a bed or sitting area. Cover them with a brightly covered cloth and put some throw pillows there. (Throw pillows could easily hide a black purse filled with jewelry and powder, as well as a mantilla!)

You'll need something to represent the pen from which Pig is freed. His face needs to be easily visible to the audience, so don't create anything very tall. It can be as elaborate as an actual wooden fence constructed by a volunteer, perhaps with a swinging gate, a cardboard fence, or simply classroom chairs pushed together to form a square.

JUAN BOBO AND THE SUNDAY PIG

Costumes

All of the people (as opposed to pigs) in this play should be dressed in their Puerto Rican Sunday best, including the Chorus. Brightly colored dresses for the ladies with shawls and of course mantillas to cover their heads. Hoop earrings can be worn in the ladies' ears. Be sure you have some costume piece, such as a brightly colored shawl, for Rosita to add for her final scene, which will make it clear that this is the present day, not the remembered day with the Pig.

Santiago would probably not wear a suit of clothes in Puerto Rico where the weather is warm, but he would surely have on a clean shirt, perhaps white, and pair of light-colored trousers.

Dress Father Fernando in black pants and a black shirt. Give him a clerical collar by cutting a length of white cardboard about a half-inch thick and thread it underneath his collar. You could age Father Fernando a bit, if you like, with some baby powder at his temples.

What fun to create the Pig costume! Start with a pink or brown outfit of sweat clothing. A hooded sweat top would be ideal—you'll just need to make little pig ears out of brown or pink construction paper and attach them to the hood with staples or safety pins. Make a "pig nose" out of one of the egg holders cut from a cardboard egg carton with two nostrils painted on the end in a piggy fashion. Attach elastic to the sides with staples to stretch around your actor's head to hold the nose in place. Make a curly tail out of pipe cleaners (or curling ribbon!) and attach it to the seat of his pants. Now, when Pig runs offstage to roll in the mud, have several stagehands ready with pieces of felt cut in the shapes of mud splatters, with double stick tape rolled up on the back, ready to stick the felt onto Rosita's dress that Pig is wearing. (Actual mud or brown paint could get awfully messy, unless you have twin dresses, one of which has been painted to look like mud and then allowed to dry. A quick change for Pig— but quite authentic looking!) Have face paint or theatrical make-up ready to smudge his face with brown.

JUAN BOBO AND THE SUNDAY PIG

(The play begins outside of a church, stage right. JUANITA and MARTINA are meeting for Sunday Mass. Their heads are covered with mantillas, and they are wearing their best dresses.)

Juanita   Good morning, Martina!

Martina   ¡Buenos días, Juanita! How are you today on this fine Sunday morning?

Juanita   I am fine, friend, and yourself?

Martina   All is well at my house. I am alone at church, today, however. Our burro stumbled and hurt his foot, so my husband Ricardo must stay home and see to him!

Juanita   I am sorry to hear this!

Martina   Not as sorry as our burro! Where is your husband today?

Juanita   Santiago will be along. He is cleaning up, washing his face from a morning of work in the fields.

Martina   *(Looking around as though looking for someone)* Juanita . . . I am looking to my left and I am looking to my right . . .

Juanita   Someone is missing! A friend of ours is not joining us on the steps of the church!

Martina   Where is Rosita? She never misses Mass . . .

Juanita   And she is never late . . .

Martina   Unless of course, her son . . .

Juanita   Oh no! Do you think more trouble could have been caused by . . .

Both   Juan Bobo?!

Martina   Oh, do not say it, Juanita! We should not make fun of the poor boy. He cannot help it if he . . . that is . . .

Juanita   He makes choices that . . .

Martina   He doesn't always do the right . . .

© 1999 by Incentive Publications, Inc.
Nashville, TN

JUAN BOBO AND THE SUNDAY PIG

Both He is a FOOL!

Juanita Poor Rosita! Ever since her husband passed away, she has had her hands full with the farm . . . and Juan Bobo!

Martina I think he means well . . .

(Enter FATHER FERNANDO, the priest.)

Father Fernando Good morning, ladies! How lovely to see you today!

Juanita Good morning, Father!

Martina Good morning, Father Fernando!

Father Fernando But one of your friends is not here? Where is Rosita?

Juanita Well, Father, we do not know for sure, but we think she may be having a problem at her home.

Father Fernando *(Holding up his hand)* I understand completely. I suppose I should recite the usual "Juan Bobo" prayer?

Martina I think it would be a good idea.

Father Fernando Very well. I will see you ladies inside the church!

(Exits)

Juanita Poor Rosita! Do you remember the time she left for Mass . . .

Martina And told Juan Bobo to watch over the farm?

Juanita Yes! Her crops had been bountiful and she was most eager to give thanks . . .

(As MARTINA and JUANITA reminisce, ROSITA and JUAN BOBO enter, stage left.)

Rosita Now, Juan Bobo, I am going to la iglesia.

Juan Bobo Sí, Mamacita! How beautiful you look! Is that your best dress?

Rosita No, Juan Bobo, this is not my very best dress. My very best dress is _____ *(insert dress color here)*. I save it for the most special occasions!

JUAN BOBO AND THE SUNDAY PIG

Juan Bobo   But Mamacita, you are not even wearing any jewelry, and yet you look as beautiful as the stars in the night sky!

Rosita   My, Juan Bobo, what flowery words you have for your mother this morning! No, I am not so vain as to wear my jewelry to church. It might seem as if I am trying to be grand! Besides, I am afraid I might lose an earring, or break one of my collares when I bow my head to pray. No, all of my jewelry is safe and sound in my black purse!

Juan Bobo   Well, good-bye, Mother! I will see you when you return!

Rosita   Now, Juan Bobo, listen to me well. I want you to take good care of the farm while I am gone. Don't do anything . . . that is, please be careful not to . . .

Juan Bobo   Do not worry about a thing, Mamacita! I will feed the duck and the pig!

Rosita   But do not feed them too much, Juan Bobo, and do not feed them foolishly!

Juan Bobo   I would never!

Rosita   Once you tried to feed a pork chop to the pig!

Juan Bobo   How was I to know he would not like pork? I love it!

Rosita   It is different for the pig.

Juan Bobo   Whatever you say, Mamacita. I will take good care.

Rosita   Do not attempt to carry water in a basket.

Juan Bobo   I will not do that . . . again.

Rosita   Do not set any fire.

Juan Bobo   I will not set any fire. Especially not in the house.

Rosita   Do not attempt to fasten the chickens into the tree with string. It will not hold.

Juan Bobo   I will not do these things. Now, off with you, Mother! You do not want to keep Father Fernando waiting!

JUAN BOBO AND THE SUNDAY PIG

Rosita *(Exiting)* All right, Juan Bobo, my son! I am trusting you!

Juan Bobo Good-bye! *(Waving good-bye to his mother as she leaves)* Now, I am in charge of the farm! Hmmm, I wonder what I should do. I think I will go see about our fine pig!

(He exits, as JUANITA and MARTINA begin to speak stage right.)

Martina So Rosita left to come to church, feeling quite afraid of what might happen.

Juanita I remember she was not at ease all morning!

(Enter SANTIAGO, JUANITA's husband.)

Santiago Hello, ladies! Let's go in and get a good seat!

Juanita No, husband! We are waiting for Rosita.

Santiago For Rosita? Mother of Juan Bobo? Oh no! I can only imagine what has happened now!

Martina We were just remembering the day Juan Bobo was left to take care of el puerquito . . .

Santiago That poor pig!

Martina Poor pig, and poor Rosita! Because the minute she left the house, Juan Bobo went out to tend to the pig . . .

(JUAN BOBO re-enters left, this time at the pen of PIG.)

Juan Bobo Hello my fine puerquito! How are you this Sunday morning?

(PIG squeals.)

Juan Bobo You are squealing! Are you hungry? *(Looks in PIG's feeding trough)* No, your trough is full. Do you need water? *(Looks in PIG's water bowl)* No, it looks like you have plenty of water. Hmmm, what could be the matter?

(PIG continues to squeal, most agitated.)

Juan Bobo You are not hungry . . . you are not thirsty . . . and yet you squeal on. There can be only one answer. You want to go to church with my mother!

JUAN BOBO AND THE SUNDAY PIG

(PIG looks out at the audience and makes a face as if to say, "What in the world?")

Juan Bobo That must be it. And of course a pig should be allowed to go to Mass just like everyone else! Come on out!

(JUAN BOBO opens the door to the pin, while the PIG looks at the audience with a much happier look on his face.)

Juan Bobo Come out, Pig! And follow me to the house.

(PIG looks confused.)

Juan Bobo You do not think that I can let you go to Father Fernando's fine church looking like that, do you? Come into my mother's bedroom, puerquito, and we will get you ready for church!

(A confused PIG and JUAN BOBO head for the house portion of the acting area.)

Santiago I will never forget Rosita telling us that Juan Bobo led that pig right into their home!

Martina And right into her bedroom . . .

Juanita Where he pulled out her best dress!

Juan Bobo Now let me see, which one did my mother say was her best dress? Oh yes, I remember! She said it was the _____ *(insert color here)* one! And oh, Pig, isn't it a fine dress! How lovely it will look on you!

(JUAN BOBO puts the dress on the confused, struggling PIG.)

Juan Bobo You will be the best-dressed pig in Mass this morning! You look . . .

(PIG strikes a pose.)

Juan Bobo You look nice, but not quite beautiful enough.

(Snaps his fingers)

Juan Bobo I know! You need jewelry! Now where did she say she kept . . . ah yes! Her black purse!

(Produces it)

JUAN BOBO AND THE SUNDAY PIG

Juan Bobo   Here are aretes for your fine piggy ears, and some lovely collares.

(Adorning the PIG with necklaces)

Juan Bobo   Now let me look at you.

(Digs in handbag)

Juan Bobo   Aha! *(Withdraws bracelets)* Brazaletes!

(Puts them on PIG and admires his handiwork. PIG is starting to look uncomfortable. JUAN BOBO claps his hands.)

Juan Bobo   Beautiful! Almost . . . what is missing! Ah!

(Produces some facial powder)

Juan Bobo   Make-up!

(Powders PIG's face with white powder)

Juan Bobo   There! Now you are fit for Mass! Off you go! Wait!

(The PIG was just about to make a run for it, but now stops.)

Juan Bobo   I am the silliest boy in Puerto Rico! What am I thinking? This isn't proper for a pig . . . you don't have a mantilla!

(Produces a mantilla and puts it on PIG.)

Juan Bobo   Now be gone! Before you miss the whole Mass!

(PIG rushes out and JUAN BOBO exits too. While PIG is offstage, he is made "muddy" and loses all jewelry. He re-enters and begins to roll about, as if in the mud, while the folks at the church talk.)

Juanita   Poor Rosita! That pig headed straight for the nearest mudhole!

Martina   *(Laughing)* I don't suppose pigs enjoy jewelry and dresses!

Santiago   Poor dear Rosita.

Martina   Can you imagine how her heart must have stopped when she was walking home from Mass . . .

JUAN BOBO AND THE SUNDAY PIG

Juanita Hurrying home, no doubt . . .

Martina Knowing that SOMETHING must have gone wrong . . .

Santiago Only to meet up with her best dress . . . in a mud puddle . . .

Juanita & Martina ON A PIG!!

(Enter ROSITA, who rushes up upon PIG wallowing in the mud.)

Rosita *(Gasps)* Puerquito! What are you . . . why do you have . . . is that my . . . JUAN BOBO!

(She exits quickly.)

Pig Maybe this dress really wasn't my color.

(Exits)

Santiago You could hear the sound of her cries all the way into the next village.

Juanita On that Sunday, she swore that she would never leave Juan Bobo alone again!

Martina I wonder if she decided to try again today?

Father Fernando *(Re-entering)* I think you should all take your seats, friends. I am afraid Rosita may not arrive in time for Mass this morning.

Martina Could we wait just a moment, Father? She is never late!

Juanita Just a few moments more?

Father Fernando Well, I . . .

(ROSITA enters, wearing a shawl to show that this is a different day than the one the friends were remembering.)

Rosita I'm so sorry I'm late, Father Fernando. But you see, my son, Juan Bobo . . .

Santiago Oh no!

Rosita *(As they head into the church)* I'll explain everything after Mass. You see, we have a duck, and a jug of molasses.

JUAN BOBO AND THE SUNDAY PIG

**Martina, Juanita,
Santiago,
& Father Fernando** Oh, Juan Bobo!

Father Fernando Goodbye, everyone! Thank you for coming!

Juan Bobo Would you like me to watch your farm?

(The CAST and CHORUS assemble onstage to sing:)

(See music page 84)

ALL HELLO FRIENDS, WE SING FOR YOU
A LITTLE SONG YOU KNOW IS TRUE
ABOUT A BOY WHO DOES NOT THINK
HIS BRAIN MUST BE ON THE BLINK!

JUAN BOBO, JUAN BOBO
THE SILLIEST BOY ANYWHERE
HE MAKES HIS MOTHER WORRY SO!
HE MAKES HER TEAR HER HAIR.

LISTEN WHILE WE TELL THE TALE
HE SET A FIRE IN THE MILK PAIL
'OH!' SAYS MOTHER, 'SUCH A MESS!'
HE DRESSED THE PIG IN HER BEST DRESS!

JUAN BOBO, JUAN BOBO
THE SILLIEST BOY ANYWHERE
HE MAKES FATHER FERNANDO
SAY A SPECIAL PRAYER!

Multicultural Plays

JUAN BOBO AND THE SUNDAY PIG

Juan Bobo

Words by Judy Truesdell Mecca

Music by Judy Truesdell Mecca and
Jenifer Truesdell Christman

The Clever Trickster Anansi

(Based on Spider Stories from Africa)

The Clever Trickster Anansi

CAST

Villagers, including:

Da

Nkatee

Kindai

Storyteller

Anansi

Sky God

Aso, Anansi's Wife

Onini, the Python

Momboro, the Hornet

Osebo, the Leopard

The Clever Trickster Anansi

Notes to the Teacher/Director

The mischievous character Anansi has long been the hero of African folklore. He is a clever, tricky spider who would much rather eat than work—yet he is good-hearted and is a well-loved folk character. (Perhaps we all see a little bit of ourselves in the scoundrel!) Storytelling was an important part of West African life. Through the stories, lessons were taught to the young people of the village. Sometimes prayers would be said prior to the telling of the story around a fire in the heart of the village. The story-teller was sometimes a man of the village, sometimes a woman.

The "Spider Stories" about Anansi's adventures began in West Africa. The Akan-speaking people called him Ananse, the Tshi-speaking people called him Anansi, as he is called in our play. The stories about this mischievous scamp traveled to the New World with the slaves. In the Caribbean, they are told as "Anancy Stories." In Jamaica, "Annancy;" and America, they became "Aunt Nancy" stories and eventually evolved into the "Brer Rabbit" stories told by people in the American South for many years.

In days when children were denied an education, oral communication was one of few available outlets. Stories provided a sense of heritage and pride to the young listeners, as well as an opportunity to share religious experiences.

Our play offers young people an opportunity to take part dramatically in a tale of Brother Anansi. In early days, the storyteller would act out all the parts, changing his or her voice to fit each character. For our purposes, boys and girls will act out the parts of Anansi and his friends.

The Villagers can be as few as three people or as large a group as you would like. In early storytelling days, the listeners would chant "Yoo-ooo-oo!" to show approval. They would answer questions posed by the Storyteller. The Villagers in our play are similarly involved in the story. They are not just sitting and listening—they are taking part and helping to advance the plot along.

Multicultural Plays

The Clever Trickster Anansi

The first part of the play is to be "ad-libbed." That is, your Villagers should casually walk around and talk between themselves as their characters would. It should be orchestrated so they will end up in the circle, awaiting the Storyteller. You may wish to discuss the difference between the scripted parts of the play and the less structured portion at the beginning.

A little artistic license has been taken with the ending. In most versions of this story, Anansi hands over the beasts to the Sky God and goes about his way, happy to have the stories. In our play, we portray Anansi asking the Sky God to release the captured animals, saying that he has tricked them and wishes them to come to no harm. Although this is not exactly true to the original folk tale, it seems to teach a nicer moral about using friends for personal gain.

The cast members who are playing animals should be encouraged to emulate real animals' movements. Are videotapes available to view the slithering movements of the python? If your audience can see him, it would be fun if Onini the Python never stands up, but just slithers along on the floor. (Please mop the day of the show!) Can a trip to the zoo be arranged to watch the muscular strength of the graceful Panther? Maybe the whole class needs to buzz around and portray hornets to help that actor (or actress) capture Momboro's nervous tiny movements.

And how would a being with eight legs deal with those extra limbs? Is Anansi quick or deliberate in his motion?

Will your class enjoy portraying the story of the how Anansi acquired the Sky God's stories? Yoo-ooo-ooo!

A little more information . . .

West Africa Today

The "Spider Stories" about the mischievous Anansi began in West Africa. Let's take a look at West Africa today—is it a very different place than it was when the storytellers gathered villagers around the fire for a tale?

The area to which we refer as "West Africa" covers about one fourth of the whole continent, but about one-third of the entire population of Africa lives here. The largest and most heavily populated country is Nigeria. Many different ethnic groups of people live in West Africa. In older days, we would have referred to them as "tribes."

West Africa includes a wide variety of languages (hundreds are spoken!), geographic conditions, and lifestyles. Although most of the people live in rural areas, not everyone farms. Many are involved in education, or are doctors, writers, weavers, or traders. In many cases, the geography of the area determines the lifestyle of the people who live there. For instance, those people trying to live off of the dry desert lands have developed a nomadic lifestyle. That is, they roam around, traveling with their herds in search of water or pasture land. The soil of most West African farms is only rich enough to support crops for the family living on that farm. In recent years, however, larger farms and plantations have begun to grow export crops such as coffee, cocoa beans, and peanuts.

Because such a huge variety of lifestyles and cultures exist throughout this vast area, it would take many chapters to give a good peek at the country. However, since Nigeria is the largest and most densely populated country, let's see if we can get a feel for what Nigerian life is like.

Many people live in big cities and enjoy many modern comforts—such as super-markets, movie theatres, department stores, and even fast food! They drive automobiles to work, get in traffic jams, and enjoy a television program or two when they get home to their apartments.

In many smaller Nigerian towns, life is more similar to the days of old. The marketplace is the center of all activity. Women bring cloth or pottery to sell, or a few vegetables from the farm. A woman might carry a huge pot balanced on her head, full of goat's milk. Home is a small hut made from mud or clay. Women cook outside the house on open fires.

Some traditions involving Nigerian marriage might surprise you! For instance, some marriages are traditional, while in other groups men have several wives. Before a woman gets married, she is kept in a "fattening room" where she is given a lot of food to eat and very little exercise. She is considered much more beautiful if she is fat. On her wedding day, her hair is piled high upon her head and made stiff with palm oil, charcoal and clay, and she wears brass spirals around her legs and ankles.

Music, art, and dance are all important parts of Nigerian culture, and come together in celebrations and religious ceremonies. In many areas, the whole village takes part in a dance, with costumes and masks and even fire as part of the celebration. There are many unique musical instruments, varying with each ethnic group, many of which are percussion instruments. The Yoruban people, for instance, have a drum known as the dundun. This instrument is called the "talking drum" because it makes such a wide variety of sounds. It is made from a solid piece of wood, open at the top with the skin of an animal stretched over it.

Our brief overview of this interesting part of the world, then, has shown us that although many areas have not changed so much since the days of the Anansi stories, many West African cities are like any other modern, fast-paced cities of the world. One thing is certain, however—West Africa continues to be an area of wide variety, rich culture, and multi-ethnic tradition.

The Clever Trickster Anansi

A recipe . . .

PETE'S YAM MASH

What You'll Need:
   6 medium-sized yams
   3 tablespoons butter or margarine
   ¼ teaspoon ginger
   ⅛ teaspoon ground cloves
   2 tablespoons sugar
   2 tablespoons brown sugar
   ½ cup milk or water

   Large cooking pot, big enough to hold six yams
   Large bowl
   Potato masher
   Fork for testing yams
   Butter knife for peeling yams
   Measuring cups and spoons
   Stirring spoons

How to make it:
   Wash yams thoroughly. Do not peel.
   Put yams in pot and cover with water (make sure there is about an inch above the
      yams).
   Bring water to boil; reduce heat to medium and continue cooking until yams can be
      pierced with fork (about 45 minutes).
   Remove yams from water and let sit just until cool enough to touch.
   Peel yams and place in large bowl.
   Using potato masher, mash thoroughly.
   Add butter, water, sugars, and spices and mash everything together.
   Serve immediately—and enjoy!

The Clever Trickster Anansi

Props

- Hand props for Villagers to carry in opening scene, including dolls, toys, cool drinks out of jars or gourds, etc.
- Storyteller's stick
- Anansi's umbrella or cloth to shield his head from the sun
- Anansi's web (See Scenery.)
- Aso's cooking tools—a bowl, wooden spoon, two plates, and spoons for Anansi's supper (You can pantomime the actual food or mix up something to represent yam mash and plantain.)
- A palm branch (or bamboo stick)
- Something to represent "creeper vines"—try green florist tape, artificial ivy, a slender rope spray-painted green or green yarn
- Something to represent Anansi's big hollowed-out gourd. Could one be fashioned out of papier mâché? Or, if Momboro is a small actor, could it be a large ceramic pot? You could also secure some foam from a florist supply house and, pinching the edges together with spray adhesive, fashion the shape of a gourd and spray paint it—floral spray works best on foam. (Because several characters comment that Anansi is carrying a gourd, your prop really only needs to suggest it.)
- A little "gourd" to hold Anansi's water.
- A big "plantain leaf" that covers Anansi's face first, when he is hiding, and later can be used to slap over the opening of the gourd. You could easily make this out of green construction paper or brown paper that has been painted green and cut in the shape of a leaf.
- A shovel
- Many leaves to cover the hole that will trap Osebo. Use real leaves or have the class cut various sizes and shapes out of construction paper.
- A large box to act as a cage. (See Scenery.)
- Two bamboo sticks or palm branches for Osebo's "ladder"
- The "story pouch" that Sky God gives Anansi at the end

Scenery

You may wish to have a wooden or wicker stool on which Storyteller may sit during the longer Anansi scenes.

Get creative when you present the illusion of Anansi spinning a web up to the Sky God! Perhaps the teacher can clear his or her desk to represent the Sky God's court. Make a "web" for Anansi out of various strands of yarn tied together, and have him pack it in a brown or black "fanny pack" or other pouch on his hip. Then, when it's time to spin the web, he unzips the pack and begins to pull out the yarn a little at a time. Affix part of it to the floor—perhaps a Villager holds it, or assists Anansi with some sturdy masking tape. Then, have him affix the other end to the edge of the teacher's desk/Sky God's court, also with tape or with a pre-positioned plastic hook (if you won't get in too much trouble for defacing school property!) Perhaps all the strands of the web are tied to a plastic loop and secured by the hook. Maybe someone's grandma has a light-colored shawl that is loose enough in its weave to represent a spider's beautiful web. You might consider Halloween spider webs from the party supply store, or cheesecloth from a fabric or hardware store. Fishing net from a bait store might work as well. Keep in mind that, whatever you choose to do, you will need to remove the web when Anansi exits the Sky God's court.

Or—you may wish to make things simple and have Anansi pantomime the weaving of the web. Sometimes a little imagination goes a long way!

You'll need a table and two chairs for the scene in which Aso serves Anansi his supper. Perhaps it would be a good idea to have the table and chairs permanently in one portion of your acting area to represent their home.

In the scene in which Momboro is captured, Anansi is described as climbing a tree. If you like, simply affix some branches (construction paper will do fine) to the back of a chair and have Anansi climb up onto the seat of the chair. Now he's up higher to sprinkle Momboro. Once again, the Storyteller is describing Anansi's actions, so your scenery only needs to support what the audience is already imagining. The large gourd can be "hidden" behind the makeshift tree so that it appears that Momboro cannot see it. Anansi can hide behind the same "tree" when Osebo the Leopard comes along.

It will be up to your actors to pantomime Osebo's capture. You can help create the illusion by putting some space between Osebo and Anansi and by having them call in loud voices to each other as though one of them was in the bottom of a deep hole. It will help, also, to have Anansi standing up on a chair, perhaps a different one than your tree chair. As for the "cage," your class will have to be on alert for a big box—a refrigerator box would be more than big enough, but other appliances such as dishwashers, stoves, etc. will be fine as well. You need not attempt to create bars around the whole cage—just cut a large square and affix strips of black construction paper to represent bars. Or, if you're handy with scissors, cut the box in such a way as to leave the cardboard in the shape of bars over the hole. Have your class decorate the outside of the box with painted-on leaves, vines, etc.—Anansi would surely want it to blend in with the forest!

Costumes

Although it would be fine to perform this play with the Villagers and Storyteller in modern dress, it would be beautiful and colorful to investigate native costuming. The women wore full, colorful skirts with wide swatches of fabric binding their babies to their backs. Bright turbans wrapped around their hair, and beads decorated their necks. Men wore long flowing robes and sandals or bare feet. The Storyteller should be the most vibrant of all, perhaps in vivid purple pants or a red skirt.

Anansi should be dressed in dark brown or black, maybe sweat clothing or some other loose fitting pants and a long sleeved T-shirt. He also needs to have four additional appendages! Perhaps a parent will cut "arms" out of fabric and sew them onto his costume, adding dark garden gloves at the end of each arm. (Make sure Anansi wears a pair on his own original hands.) Pad him with pillows or other soft stuffing. Now—it's up to you and your cast whether or not Anansi has a tiny waist. This is supposedly the first Anansi story, because it is the account of how there came to be Anansi stories. In a later tale, Anansi is tripped up by his own greed and, by trying to get to two different feasts at the same time, has ropes around his waist that grow tighter and tighter until he has a very tiny waist. (This is the folk explanation for why spiders have tiny waists.) Strictly speaking, this has not happened yet when this story takes place—but if you want to create the illusion of the spider's tiny waist by cinching him in with a belt, you'll probably be forgiven.

How would a Sky God appear?! Would he wear the bright colors of the sun or the blues of the sky? Would his face be concealed behind a large, brightly colored mask? There are no rules here! Let your class decide.

Aso's costume should be the female version of Anansi's, except perhaps with an apron and maybe some beads or a turban.

The three captured creatures offer opportunities for creativity as well. Dress Onini the Python in gray and black—perhaps sweat clothing or a T-shirt and pants. Perhaps a hooded jacket could be worn—and perhaps a snaky tongue could be cut out of felt and attached to the chin. You might want to experiment with face paints. Check out a book from the library that shows the python's markings and, using theatrical make-up or a face-painting kit, let your actor make his face to look like Brother Onini.

Momboro the Hornet must surely be dressed in brown and gold colors with a menacing stinger attached to his or her behind! You can create the stinger from construction paper or soft foam from the fabric store. Antennae can be fashioned out of pipe cleaners and attached with bobby pins or glued to a plastic headband.

Osebo the Leopard must be spotted. Perhaps your actor or actress can sacrifice a pair of gold or tan sweats and allow you to paint brown spots all over them. If not, construction paper or felt circles could be pinned on temporarily. This would be another fun opportunity to do some creative make-up. Examine a photograph of a leopard and see how closely it can be matched with face paints.

 © 1999 by Incentive Publications, Inc. Nashville, TN

The Clever Trickster Anansi

(The play begins in the middle of a West African village, just at sundown. VILLAGERS are milling around, ending their day, calling greetings to one another. Boys and girls run and play with little boats or dolls or chase each other; women bounce their babies bound to their backs with brightly colored bolts of fabric; men drink cool drinks. Gradually, they begin to form a circle, sitting down. They begin to speak among themselves, "Is it time for a story yet?" "Call the storyteller!" Soon the STORYTELLER enters. Greeting one and all, he or she walks to the center of the circle, then beats the ground sharply with a stick.)

Storyteller   Gather 'round, people of my village! There is a story in my head trying to get out of my mouth! Will you hear it?

Da   Of course we will hear it!

Nkatee   Story time at last! After such a hard day's work.

Storyteller   Perhaps you would like a story about someone very clever?

Villagers   Yoo-ooo-ooo!

Storyteller   Someone who is lazy, but enjoys a good meal!

Villagers   Yes! Yes!

Storyteller   We have shared many stories about him already. Perhaps you are tired of hearing about . . . Anansi the Spider!

Villagers   No, no, never!

Kindai   We can never hear too many stories about the tricky Anansi!

Storyteller   But many, many stories are told about Anansi. Why is this, do you suppose, Villagers? Why are so many stories shared around a fire on a moonlit night like this—about a lazy spider who hides from honest work?

Da   Tell us, Storyteller! How did Anansi stories begin?

Storyteller   This is the story you would like to hear tonight?

The Clever Trickster Anansi

Villagers   Yoo-ooo-ooo!

Storyteller   Then here it is. I do not know whether this is the truth, but I think it may be. Once, long ago, all the stories were owned by the great Sky God, and they were not told on Earth. Anansi the Spider grew jealous! He wanted all people everywhere to tell stories of his great adventures.

(Enter ANANSI, who is carrying an umbrella or cloth to shield his head from the sun.)

Villagers   *(In unison)* YOO-OOO-OOO ANANSI! LAZY, HUNGRY ONE! YOO-OOO-OOO ANANSI! HIDING FROM THE SUN!

Anansi   The sun is bright today! Too bright for a tiny spider who could easily burn up! I must rest in the shade of this palm tree and think about what to do next.

Storyteller   Anansi loves to sit and think almost as much as he loves a big meal!

Anansi   It is a hot afternoon and I do not have anything to eat. How I wish I could sit in the shade of this tree and hear a story. A wonderful story about trickery and cleverness. A story about my favorite subject—ME!

Storyteller   But can he hear such a story?

Villagers   *(In unison)* NO HE CANNOT!

Storyteller   But why?

Villagers   *(In unison)* BECAUSE ALL THE STORIES ARE IN THE SKY.

Storyteller   That is right! The powerful Sky God owned all the stories. But this did not stop Anansi.

The Clever Trickster Anansi

Anansi I know that the webs I spin are the most beautiful in the land. But that does not satisfy me any longer! I want to spin wonderful stories, too, for all to hear! There must be a way to take the stories from the Sky God.

Villagers *(In unison)* A WAY, A WAY TO STEAL STORIES TODAY THERE MUST BE A WAY TO STEAL THEM AWAY

Anansi I will go and visit the Sky God! I will be properly humble and bow down to him. I will ask him to give me his stories!

Storyteller So Anansi began to spin a web. He spun and he spun until he had a web high enough to reach the sky, to reach the court of the Sky God.

(After ANANSI has spun his web up to his court, the SKY GOD enters.)

Sky God Who dares to approach the court of Nyami, the Sky God?!

Anansi *(Bowing)* It is I, Anansi the Spider!

Sky God Oh, Anansi! Why have you come here today? Did you think that I had a pot of greens or yams on my stove?

Anansi No, Sky God, Great God of Everything In The World!

Sky God Oh no. He must really want something!

Anansi It is true, there is one little thing I want.

Sky God And that is?

Anansi I want to buy your stories from you.

Sky God Buy my stories?! Are you mad?

Anansi No, oh Sky God! I will give you whatever want!

Sky God Oh, Anansi! Greater, more powerful beings than you have tried to buy my stories! You are so tiny! How can you expect to pay the price?

Anansi I can do it. I am Anansi.

Sky God Very well, little Anansi, here is the price for my stories. Bring me Onini, the Python; Momboro, the Hornet; and Osebo the Leopard.

Anansi I will do as you ask.

Sky God I will not hold my breath.

(ANANSI "climbs down his web" and SKY GOD exits.)

Storyteller What do you think, my friends? Will the Spider Anansi be able to deliver these three fierce creatures to the Sky God?

Villagers *(In unison)* Never!

Storyteller Will he be able to trap these animals without being eaten up himself?

Villagers *(In unison)* No! Never!

Storyteller But he IS the cunning little spider Anansi who has been known to pull a trick or two. Can he do this?

Villagers *(In unison)* No! No! Never!

(A pause, then:)

Nkatee Well . . . maybe . . .

Storyteller We shall see! Anansi rushed home to his good wife, Aso, who was cooking plantain and yam mash for their supper.

Aso Oh no, Anansi, you have that look in your eye again.

The Clever Trickster Anansi

Anansi What look is that, Aso?

Aso That "I'm-going-to-do-something-really-impossible-to-get-my-way" look.

Anansi Aso, my good wife who loves me so much . . .

Aso Uh oh.

Anansi I have struck a deal with the Sky God!

Aso Did he come to visit you under your palm tree?

Anansi No, I visited him! And I offered to buy his stories from him that they may belong to me and I will be the most famous spider in all of the world!

Aso What price does he ask? We are a poor family!

Anansi Well . . . the first thing I must do is capture Onini the Python.

Aso *(Sarcastically)* Oh, is that all? I thought it would be something difficult!

Anansi Surely there is a way!

Aso Well, yes, I think there is. First, you must cut a sturdy palm branch and some tough vine-creeper. Then, here is what you must do, husband.

(ASO pantomimes whispering in Anansi's ear while STORYTELLER speaks.)

Storyteller And, like many a wife still does, Aso gave Anansi a good suggestion.

Anansi Great idea, Aso! I'm so glad I thought of it!

(As ANANSI exits excitedly, ASO looks at the audience and shrugs her shoulders.)

Multicultural Plays

The Clever Trickster Anansi

Aso Sometimes you must give them a little push in the right direction. *(She exits.)*

(ANANSI re-enters, carrying the palm branch and vines as the VILLAGERS chant:)

Villagers *(In unison)* OH BROTHER ANANSI!
             NOW HE MUST TRAP A SNAKE
             OH BROTHER ANANSI!
             PLEASE, DON'T MAKE A MISTAKE!

Storyteller Anansi walked down to the river where he spotted Brother Python relaxing in the sun.

(ONINI enters and reclines.)

Storyteller He gulped . . .

Anansi Gulp!

Storyteller And walked nearer to Onini.

Anansi *(Talking to himself)* No, I just don't think she's right. I must speak to my wife and tell her that she doesn't know anything about snakes!

Onini *(Looking up)* Who goes there?

Anansi No, it just can't be! Now that I look at him, I know that my wife is completely wrong!

Onini Anansi, you noisy little spider, is that you? I'm resting here!

Anansi Forgive me Brother Onini, I was just talking to myself.

Onini *(To audience)* I guess no one else will listen.

Anansi About you.

The Clever Trickster Anansi

Onini *(Interested now)* About me?

Anansi Yes, it was something my wife said about you. But I'm sure you don't want to hear it.

Onini *(Coming near to ANANSI)* What did the good Aso say about me?

Anansi I am quite sure it isn't true!

Onini Anansi, if you don't tell me what she said this minute you will be the side dish of my next meal.

Anansi Well, I hate to tell you for fear that you will think my wife foolish, but . . . she thinks that this palm branch is longer than you. *(Displaying the branch for ONINI to see)*

Onini This palm branch here?

Anansi This very one!

Onini She thinks that I am shorter than this branch?

Anansi I'm afraid she does!

(Onini starts to giggle, then builds up to a full laugh. ANANSI joins him. They laugh uproariously together.)

Anansi I told her it was ridiculous. But, Onini, would you allow me to . . . oh never mind.

Onini No, what would you like? I do not know when I have enjoyed such a laugh, Anansi! I am in your debt.

Anansi Well, that I may tell her just how foolish she is, will you allow me to lay the branch next to you on the ground and compare your length to it?

Onini Of course, Anansi! Little payment for such a good laugh.

Multicultural Plays

(ONINI reclines and ANANSI puts the palm branch next to him. Swiftly, as ONINI gasps and makes surprised comments, ANANSI binds him to the branch with the vine-creepers which he has produced. As he does this, the VILLAGERS chant:)

Villagers *(In unison)* ANANSI, ANANSI!
THAT BRANCH LOOKS RATHER TEENY
LYING ON THE GROUND
NEAR THE MIGHTY SNAKE, ONINI!
ANANSI, ANANSI!
YOU LIVE A LUCKY LIFE
YOU ARE SURELY LUCKY
TO HAVE ASO AS YOUR WIFE!

Anansi Now, Brother Python, I will deliver you to the Sky God! And thank you! The idea that a tiny little spider could outwit a huge mighty snake like yourself has provided me with a most excellent laugh today! Now come along!

(ONINI and ANANSI exit. ANANSI pantomimes dragging ONINI offstage as ONINI grumbles and vows revenge.)

Storyteller *(As ASO re-enters)* Anansi put Onini in a safe place, made sure he was securely tied and went home once more to his good wife Aso.

Aso So, is Brother Python captured? Do you own the Sky God's stories?

Anansi He is captured, good wife, he is! But there is more to my bargain with the Sky God. I must eat yams and plantain while I think of a way to trap Momboro, the hornet!

Aso *(Serving him his meal)* Oh, this gets better and better. Momboro, you say. Hmmm. I think this might work. Go out behind our hut and take the largest gourd you can find. Then . . .

(ASO pantomimes telling ANANSI how to catch the hornet while STORYTELLER speaks.)

The Clever Trickster Anansi

Storyteller   As Anansi enjoyed a fine feast, Aso gave him a good plan for catching Momboro, the Hornet. He became so excited that he jumped up from the table and left half of his yams uneaten! This had never happened before in their home!

Aso   *(Looking at the half-eaten bowl as ANANSI jumps up.)* Husband, are you ill with a fever?

Anansi   No, wife, I am ill with the desire to catch a hornet! And I think I may know just how to do it!

Aso   *(As ANANSI exits)* I am lucky to have such a clever husband—who is a good listener!

Villagers   *(In unison)* BUZZ BUZZ, MOMBORO!
ANANSI IS HEADING YOUR WAY!
BUZZ BUZZ, MOMBORO!
TO TRICK YOU AND TRAP YOU TODAY!

(ANANSI re-enters, carrying a large hollowed-out "gourd" and a smaller one with water in it.)

Storyteller   Anansi walked into the forest looking for Momboro.

Anansi   I am certainly glad that I have these extra hands to carry this gourd! It is heavy!

Storyteller   *(As MOMBORO enters, buzzing)* Soon, Momboro came buzzing along. Anansi spotted him and put the gourd behind a tree. Then, the crafty spider climbed the tree and covered his face with a plantain leaf. When Momboro came close enough, Anansi threw a sprinkle of water down on the little hornet!

Momboro   Oh no! A rainstorm!

Anansi   *(Coming into MOMBORO's line of vision)* Oh no indeed! A terrible rainstorm in the middle of the forest! We shall be washed away for sure, we tiny helpless insects.

Villagers *(In unison)* Helpless? Anansi?

Anansi *(To VILLAGERS)* Be quiet, won't you? I'm trying to trick this hornet!

Momboro Anansi? Is that you?

Anansi Yes it is, friend Momboro! Whatever will we do?

Momboro Well, it may be my imagination, but the rain seems to have let up!

Anansi Oh really? Why, look over there!

(While MOMBORO is looking one way, ANANSI sneaks back to his little gourd of water and splashes MOMBORO again.)

Anansi I think it is not letting up at all, Momboro. On the contrary, I think it is growing stronger!

Momboro Oh no, we're doomed!

(ANANSI fetches his large gourd.)

Momboro Anansi, what is that?

Anansi This? Oh, this is an old hollowed-out gourd I found. I leave it in the forest in case of torrential rains like this one.

Momboro Are you going to take shelter inside it?

Anansi Well, yes, Momboro, that is what I had in mind!

Momboro Oh . . . well, it has been nice knowing you Anansi. I will surely drown.

Anansi Wait, Momboro, where are my manners? You may get inside the gourd and be protected.

The Clever Trickster Anansi

Momboro Oh, no, Anansi, I couldn't! Unless there is room for us both?

Anansi There might be. You climb in first and then I'll come in after you if there is room.

Momboro But Anansi . . .

Anansi I insist, old friend. Climb in.

Villagers BUZZ BUZZ, MOMBORO!
FLY AWAY AND QUICK!
BUZZ BUZZ MOMBORO!
IT'S ANOTHER ANANSI TRICK!

Anansi *(Snapping a wet plantain leaf over the opening of the gourd.)* I'm very sorry to say this, Momboro, but I have trapped you! I will now put you with our friend the Python until it is time to deliver you to the Sky God!

Momboro Such a stinging I will give you, Anansi, when I escape! You will swell up to the size of this gourd!

Anansi Thank you for the warning! Now off we go!

(MOMBORO and ANANSI exit. ANANSI pretends to drag MOMBORO in the gourd. ASO re-enters.)

Storyteller Once again Anansi went home to his good wife Aso—and to the rest of his yams!

(ANANSI reenters.)

Aso My Anansi! Did you trap Momboro?

Anansi Yes, Aso, yes! He is trapped in a gourd and will buzz no more until he is in the court of the Sky God! Now where is the rest of my fine meal?

Aso Here it is, husband! Now sit down and eat. *(ANANSI sits and begins to eat).* Will you be going to see the Sky God today?

Anansi I will be going soon, but there is one more thing I must do first.

Aso Why am I not surprised?

Anansi This will be the most difficult of all. I must trap—are there more yams, wife?

Aso *(Sighing, and fetching more yams.)* What else must you do, Anansi? Paint the sky red? Make the sun wink out for a whole day? Make fish fly around the forest treetops?

Anansi I must catch Osebo, the Leopard.

Aso I am getting hard of hearing, husband! I thought you just said that you, a tiny spider, were going to try to catch Osebo, the mighty leopard!

Anansi That is what I did say, wife. Now, how to do it?

Aso *(Sighing)* Why don't you try this? Go dig a big hole in the forest, then . . .

(Once again, ASO pantomimes telling ANANSI how to catch the leopard while STORYTELLER speaks.)

Storyteller Anansi listened and ate and listened and ate some more. Aso gave him a plan—it was risky, it was dangerous, but he was ready to try it!

Anansi *(Getting up from the table)* Aso, I would love to stay and chat with you, but I have to catch Osebo, the Leopard. I will be back before dark, with many stories to tell you— about ME! *(He exits.)*

The Clever Trickster Anansi

Aso I could certainly tell a few stories of my own about you, husband! *(She exits.)*

(ANANSI re-enters, carrying a shovel. He pantomimes digging a big hole and covering it with leaves, while the VILLAGERS chant:)

Villagers BE CAREFUL, BE CAREFUL, ANANSI
THE LEOPARD IS STRONG AND MEAN
BE CAREFUL, BE CAREFUL, ANANSI
KEEP WATCHING, BE CLEVER AND KEEN!

(ANANSI hides behind a tree and waits for Osebo to come by. He does, and pantomimes falling into the hole. ANANSI comes out from behind the tree.)

Anansi Look at this big hole! I should fill it in with dirt before someone falls in it!

Osebo Hello! Help! I have fallen into this hole and I can't get up!

Anansi Who is down there? Is that you, Osebo?

Osebo Yes, it is I friend Anansi! Can you help me to escape?

Anansi Yes, but I am afraid to, Osebo! I am afraid you will eat me and my whole family the minute I free you!

Osebo I will not, I promise!

Anansi You will not eat my wife? My children? My nieces and nephews?

Osebo Never!

Anansi Then I will see what I can do.

(ANANSI drags in the large box that will act as a cage. He produces two bamboo sticks or palm branches and lowers them to OSEBO. When OSEBO climbs out on this makeshift ladder, the cage is waiting. ANANSI slams the door shut behind him. OSEBO looks out the "bars.")

Multicultural Plays

The Clever Trickster Anansi

Osebo   I take it back, Anansi! I will make a nice salad out of you and all of your family members!

Anansi   I do not think you will, Osebo! You are going to the Sky God and I will tell stories about this day for years to come!

(ANANSI fetches MOMBORO and ONINI. He pantomimes dragging them all as they exit together, headed for the SKY GOD's court.)

Storyteller   So Anansi captured all three of the creatures he promised he would capture, and he delivered them to the Sky God's door.

(SKY GOD enters.)

Sky God   I don't believe it! You have trapped these fierce creatures somehow!

Anansi   Yes, God of All Things. Here are Onini the Python, Momboro the Hornet, and Osebo the Leopard in payment for your stories.

Sky God   A sky god is true to his word. Anansi, here are my stories! *(Handing ANANSI a pouch)* Take them and tell them well. From now on, they will be known as Spider Stories.

Anansi   Thank you! But there is one thing more . . .

Sky God   What else in the world could there possibly be?

Anansi   Please don't harm the creatures that I have brought you. They were tricked and mean no harm.

Sky God   What use do I have for them? I only chose them because I thought they would be impossible for you to capture. I will let them go at once.

Anansi   Thank you.

Sky God   One more thing, Anansi.

The Clever Trickster Anansi

Anansi Yes?

Sky God Please give your good wife, Aso, a message for me. Tell her that I said, "She is very clever."

Anansi *(Puzzled)* I will.

Sky God Now be gone! Tell your stories!

Storyteller Anansi raced back to his village and gathered everyone around to hear the first Anansi story, just as I have gathered you today.

(ANANSI enters the VILLAGERS' area.)

Anansi Hello, Villagers! Would you like to hear a story? The tale of how I came to be the most famous spider in all of the world?

Villagers *(In unison)* Not today, Anansi! We have already heard it!

The Tale of the DRAGON
A Play for Chinese New Year

The Tale of the DRAGON

CAST

Zhang Chi

Chen Li, her friend

Narrator

Mrs. Heu, the teacher

Mrs. Ping, Zhang Chi's mother

Mr. Zhang, Zhang Chi's father

Grandma Chih-Chien, Zhang Chi's grandmother

Gong, the dragon

Mrs. Xin (pronounced Shin), Chen Li's mother

Mr. Chen, Chen Li's father

Classmates, including:

Feng Libing

Yu Kai

Hua Dan

The Tale of the DRAGON

Notes to the Teacher/Director:

Welcome to Beijing, China!

China is the most densely populated country in the world, and its peoples' lives reflect the conditions of their land—for example, people ride bicycles rather than drive to work.

Although most of China is rural farmland, where tea and rice are grown, our play takes place in the capital city of Beijing, where people are very fortunate to have "luxurious," two bedroom apartments. There are few refrigerators, so people must shop for their food daily. Apartments face common courtyards where children play. In many cases, these apartments are offered at a very inexpensive rate by the factories that employ the adults, often both husband and wife. Children go to school early in the morning, after they have joined the family in the street or courtyard for brisk exercise. The Chinese believe in the importance of keeping physically fit. They eat lean meat, stirred with fresh strips of vegetables. Chinese boys and girls study math, science, history, physical training, political studies, geography, and art. They learn to read and write Chinese. They do "eye exercises," thought to prevent the need for glasses. (In fact, few children in China do have the need for glasses!) Many members of the family live in the same house. Most mothers work, so many grandmothers and grandfathers live in the same home and take care of the children while the parents work outside the home. Grandparents and all elderly people are respected and honored in China. Because of the crowded conditions of their country, the Chinese government encourages families to have only one child.

But no one in Zhang Chi's family cares about being crowded or living in less-than-luxurious conditions in *The Tale of the Dragon*, because Chinese New Year is coming! This joyous holiday is celebrated on days that fluctuate from year to year, some time between January 1, and February 20. A Chinese lunar calendar is used, in which each month begins with a new moon. Chinese New Year is a time of parades and feasting, of special presents for the children and good will all around. In our story, Zhang Chi's class at school has been honored by being allowed to participate in the largest parade in Beijing. Zhang Chi has received another honor— she and four other students have been selected to make and carry the paper dragon that will lead the parade. The problem is, Zhang Chi must carry the tail while her friend Chen Li gets to carry the head. Zhang Chi is sad, thinking that her part in the festivities will not be as great an honor as that of her friend, until a dragon named Gong visits her in her sleep. He explains how vital the tail support position

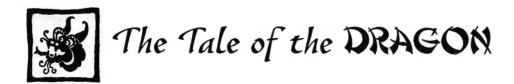

is, letting her know that his own tail is always dragging lower than the rest of him, knocking the tops off of trees, etc. He even shares that this is the reason dragons are called "dragons"—because their tails are always "draggin'"! Zhang Chi realizes that she has been silly, reconciles with her friend, and then they and their classmates lead the parade proudly through the classroom—and out into the hall or street if you like, encouraging all audience members to carry a banner or bang a drum and take part in the festivities.

In addition to the speaking roles, you may include as many classmates and parade participants as you would like. In the parade, allow your cast members to do acrobatics, play instruments, perform martial arts, dance, or sing.

The names of the characters in this play may be somewhat confusing! One difference is that the order of first and last names are reversed. Zhang Chi's given name is "Chi" and her family name is Zhang, which she shares with her father, Mr. Zhang. In China, however, many women do not adopt their husband's family name—therefore, her mother's name is Mrs. Ping. The same applies to Chen Li's family.

Have a wonderful time celebrating Chinese New Year with this play, and Kung Hey Fat Choi—May prosperity be with you!

The Tale of the DRAGON

A recipe . . .

XUCHEN'S CHINESE NEW YEAR'S CAKE

What you'll need:

½ lb. sweet rice flour
⅛ lb. regular rice flour
1 cup water
½ cup brown sugar
¼ cup sugar
2 teaspoons vegetable oil

A mixing bowl
A spoon
2 9-inch cake pans
Plastic wrap
Cellophane tape
Wok (to steam)

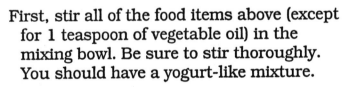

How to make it:

First, stir all of the food items above (except for 1 teaspoon of vegetable oil) in the mixing bowl. Be sure to stir thoroughly. You should have a yogurt-like mixture.

Next, line the pans with plastic wrap, and secure each edge with tape. Coat each wrap evenly with half a teaspoon of vegetable oil.

Pour the mixture made earlier into the two pans, trying to divide it evenly between the two.

Steam the mixture in a covered wok for 20-30 minutes or until it is dry. (The normal way of finding out is to stick a toothpick into it before steaming. When taken out, if nothing clings to the stick, it is dry.) Wait for it to cool, and then cut it. Enjoy!

Multicultural Plays

The Tale of the DRAGON

Props
- Books, papers, pencils for the boys and girls in their classroom
- Books for Zhang Chi and Chen Li to carry
- A deck of cards
- A few pots and pans for breakfast preparation in the Zhang apartment
- The items that will be described during the New Year's Eve celebration, including:
  - Various dishes to represent the specific foods listed (You need not have actual food in the dishes—just have something with a cover.)
  - Flowers (including something that will look like peach blossoms, if possible)
  - Fruit (including, if possible, something that will look like kumquats on a little plant)
  - Articles of red clothing for the girls
  - Red and gold envelopes for the Laisee ("lucky money")
- Various things for parade participants to carry, including:
  - Red strips of cloth which can be twirled
  - Any festively colored banners
  - Drums, gongs, or other instruments
  - The paper dragon! This will be your biggest project. Boys and girls should look at books from the library to get ideas for a design. There are various ways in which to construct the head. Students might paint a face on a piece of poster board so that the head actually looks more like a mask than a three-dimensional head. They could duplicate the design on two separate pieces of posterboard, and glue them on either side of a pole or yardstick. Fabric could be draped over the pole to mask it. A more three-dimensional look could be created by cutting a ferocious snout and teeth out of construction paper and attaching them to the poster board. Students could experiment with soft foam, forming it into the shape of a dragon head and then painting the face and features. They could also start with a hard plastic hat of some sort, so that Chen Li could actually put the hat on her head. The poster board or foam could be glued to the hat. The body could be anything from bed sheets to long, painted strips of butcher paper, but the tail should be something special. Is it a length of material, sewn and stuffed with cotton? Is it a big piece of cardboard or poster board—or several attached pieces? Whatever your cast chooses, it should coordinate with the head and be displayed proudly by your Zhang Chi!

Scenery
You'll need part of your classroom to represent the Beijing classroom for the first portion of the play. Line up as many desks as you care to include, remembering that you'll have to strike them for the Zhang family's apartment.

For the Zhang family's apartment, there should be very little furniture. Some arrangement of chairs where the family can sit and play cards, plus a table, are needed. In some Chinese apartments, the family saves space by having the children sleep in bunks that are built high, over other furnishings. They access these bunks by a ladder. This might be difficult to accomplish in your classroom, so just providing Zhang Chi a bed roll in the corner would work just as well. Remember—for realism—everything should be close and not very luxurious.

Costumes

Most people in Chinese cities dress in a modern, Western fashion. The boys and girls dress comfortably for school in pants and multi-colored shirts. (Some boys and girls in China belong to a group called "The Little Red Soldiers" or "Young Pioneers." This group is dedicated to good heath, good study, and good productive work, and it is an honor to be included. To show their membership, they wear red scarves tied around their necks. You may wish to include this as a part of Zhang Chi and Chen Li's costumes.)

The adults should be also dressed comfortably and in modern style, with the possible exception of Grandma Chih-Chien and the Narrator. Grandma Chih-Chien, frisky as she is, probably wears slacks, but maybe she wears a more traditional top with a Chinese stand-up collar. You may wish to add some baby powder to Grandma Chih-Chien's hair.

If you like, it may be fun to dress the Narrator in full traditional Chinese attire. Have your students check out books from the library to get ideas for this colorful, traditional costume. (In addition to books about China, they might also look in books about clothing of various cultures.)

You should probably make every effort to have your costume for Gong mirror the final paper dragon design for the parade, as though Zhang Chi was inspired by her "visitor." Your class will wish to visit the library for dragon design ideas—brainstorm with them about the costume for Gong. Should he or she be dressed in solid red or green, perhaps sweat clothing? A bright yellow or red sash might be a nice touch, or you might wish to go with traditional Chinese attire. As for Gong's face and head, you have choices. You could start with a baseball or other soft cap. After making sure this cap is dispensable, glue construction paper or soft foam in the shape of a dragon's long snout with ferocious teeth. Then your actor simply wears the cap with the dragon head sticking out in front. You could also purchase theatrical make-up from the party supply store and, using one of your dragon pictures as a guide, apply make-up to Gong's face.

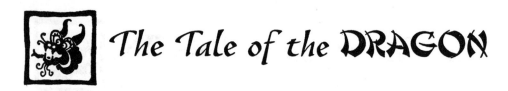

The Tale of the DRAGON

(When the play begins, we see a classroom setting. Boys and girls, including ZHANG CHI and CHEN LI are working hard, writing on tablets or reading books. Their teacher, MRS. HEU, is walking around looking at their work. The NARRATOR enters and speaks to the audience.)

Narrator Good day, everyone, and welcome to Beijing, China! Come with us as we explore and enjoy a wonderful time of year for the Chinese people—Chinese New Year! See our main character, Zhang Chi? *(Crossing to her)* She is a good and hard-working student. This is her best friend, Chen Li. *(Indicates CHEN LI.)* These girls have been best friends for as long as they can remember. Their fathers work in the same factory, and their families live in two apartments separated by a courtyard. They have no trouble running across that courtyard to see each other, believe me!

(ZHANG CHI reaches across to squeeze her friend CHEN LI's hand. They giggle briefly behind their hands and continue working before the teacher can see them.)

The girls are very excited today and are having a little trouble working. The reason is very simple—Chinese New Year is coming and they cannot wait! This is a time of celebration, of special foods, of starting . . . well, a new year! The children are given gifts—oh well, you'll see. Ooops! The teacher is talking! (He moves to the side of the acting area.)

Mrs. Heu Boys and girls, you have done excellent work today! I have some wonderful news to share with you, so give me your attention please. *(The students put down pencils, etc. and listen to their teacher.)* Do any of you realize that Chinese New Year is coming?

(The boys and girls laugh at her joke and raise their hands.)

I thought perhaps you did. What you do not know is that our school has been asked to take part in the biggest parade in town! Some boys and girls will sing, some will perform martial arts, some will do acrobatics and some will play musical instruments. But I have been asked to choose a special group of boys and girls who are talented artists and hard workers to receive a special honor. Should I tell you what it is?

(The boys and girls raise their hands again, this time a few ad-libbing "Please! Please!")

Maybe tomorrow.

(The boys and girls look upset, mistakenly taking their teacher seriously.)

I am joking with you students and I should stop. This is the special honor: A team of you will work together to build a huge paper dragon, which you will proudly hold high as you lead the parade!

(This is quite exciting news to the students, and they clap their hands and talk to each other.)

Quiet now, listen as I list the team members. It was hard to decide, but here are the boys and girls who will build and carry the dragon. Feng Libing, Yu Kai, Hua Dan . . . and let's see, are there two others? Oh yes. Zhang Chi and Chen Li!

(The boys and girls all react excitedly when their names are called and the other boys and girls pat them on the backs and congratulate them. MRS. HEU continues.)

You will all work together to build and paint the beautiful paper dragon. The first three students on the team will support the middle of Mr. Dragon as you proudly march. Chen Li, you will have the honor of carrying his mighty head, and Zhang Chi will carry—his tail! Now, boys and girls, you are dismissed for the day!

(Everyone is excited except ZHANG CHI, who looks disappointed and moves slowly to gather up her books and papers to go home. While the girls talk, the classmates quietly strike the classroom and set up the ZHANG's house.)

Chen Li *(Joining her friend and walking out of the classroom.)* Oh my friend! Isn't it wonderful! We will be working together on the beautiful dragon! What fun!

Zhang Chi Yes, it will be fun . . . especially for you!

Chen Li Whatever do you mean, Chi?

Zhang Chi Well, we will have fun painting and designing the dragon, that's true!

Multicultural Plays

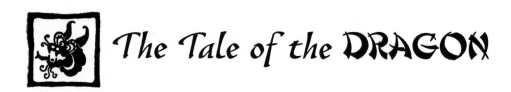

Chen Li   Of course!

Zhang Chi   And we always have a good time working together . . .

Chen Li   Always!

Zhang Chi   But Li, at the parade, you will be proudly carrying . . .

Chen Li   His head!

Zhang Chi   And where will I be?

Chen Li   You will be right there with me!

Zhang Chi   Oh no, I will not! I will not be supporting the dragon's shoulder! I will be carrying his tail, way at the back, not a position of honor at all!

Chen Li   Oh my friend, this is the silliest thing I have ever heard. We will work together, we will march together! It is an honor even to be included on the team!

Zhang Chi   Easy for someone to say who is carrying the dragon's head!

Chen Li   I cannot believe this is how you feel. I will see you at home, Zhang Chi, if you want to see me. Good-bye. *(She exits, walking fast. ZHANG CHI exits also, moving slowly and sadly.)*

(Re-entering. While he speaks, MRS. PING, MR. ZHANG and GRANDMA CHIH-CHIEN enter and take their places in the living room. They begin to play a game of cards.)

Narrator   Oh no, this is terrible! Zhang Chi should not be sad about her part of the festivities! She should never allow these feelings to come between her and her longtime friend, Chen Li! A paper dragon has come between two friends—or is it Zhang Chi? Let's see what happens when she talks to her family. These are her parents, and this is her grandmother, whom she honors very much. It is later that night, after the family has had their evening meal.

(NARRATOR exits.)

Zhang Chi   Mother, Father and Grandmother, I need to talk to you about something.

Grandma Chih-Chien   Chi, come here to your grandmother. Bring your cheek here that I may give it a little kiss.

(ZHANG CHI crosses to her grandmother and they hug. GRANDMA CHIH-CHIEN whispers in her ear:)

I am defeating your parents so badly in this game of cards that they may never play with me again! Should I let them win?

Zhang Chi   No, Grandmother, show them no mercy. Even if they decide never to play with you, I always will.

Grandma Chih-Chien   You are a wise little one, Chi, and you play a good game of cards. But not your parents! They are making me fall asleep!

Mrs. Ping   Chi, what is it? Of course you may talk to us about anything that is on your mind.

Mr. Zhang   Are you having trouble, my dear? Surely not, you are such a good student.

Zhang Chi   No, I am not having trouble with my schoolwork. In fact, I have been chosen for a great honor!

Mrs. Ping   And this news has waited until after our dinner? That isn't like you, Chi! You and Chen Li usually tell good news quickly. By the way, where is Li! Isn't she usually over to see if you can come out and play by now?

Zhang Chi   Oh, Mother. What a confusing day! My honor is wonderful and yet awful, and Li is my best friend and not my friend at all.

Mr. Zhang   I must be getting really old really fast.

Grandma Chih-Chien   No, that's not it. You're just getting beaten at cards so badly that you can't think! I understand perfectly. Something happened at school that would be wonderful but it is not quite for some reason—and it has caused trouble between the two friends and Chi feels terrible about it! *(Looking at ZHANG CHI)* How am I doing?

Zhang Chi   Grandmother, you are amazing. That is exactly right.

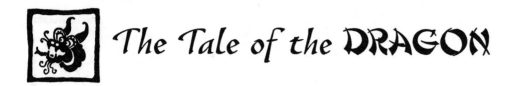

Mr. Zhang   What is your honor, my daughter?

Zhang Chi   I am chosen to help build and carry the big paper dragon for the New Year's parade!

MR. ZHANG, MRS. PING & GRANDMA CHIH-CHIEN (Ad-libbing)
How wonderful! What an honor! What happy news!

Zhang Chi   But there is one thing wrong. Chen Li gets to carry the head. And I will be carrying—I hate to say it—the dragon's tail!

(All stare at ZHANG CHI as if waiting for more information.)

Zhang Chi   Did you not hear me? His tail!

Grandma Chih-Chien   I think I must not be hearing the whole story. You get to help build the dragon . . .

Mr. Zhang   A great honor.

Grandma Chih-Chien   You get to help carry the dragon . . .

Mrs. Ping   In the New Year's parade . . .

Grandma Chih-Chien   And you're angry because Li gets to support the head, and you have the tail?

Zhang Chi   Everyone, I have always had a dream of proudly walking down the street, leading the New Year's parade, holding the head of a mighty dragon. I think of how the people will wave and how the dragon will frolic—the dragon's tail just doesn't seem the same!

Mrs. Ping   Chi, I think you have gotten confused.

Mr. Zhang   I think you will have a wonderful time!

Grandma Chih-Chien   Chi, my granddaughter, I think you are—how shall I say this—nuts!

Zhang Chi   Oh, never mind, everybody. I'll just go to bed! I can't tell you how I feel, so I'll just tell you goodnight.

Grandma Chih-Chien   Good night, dear! I'll let you know if your parents ever win a hand of cards!

(ZHANG CHI goes to her small bedroom area. She crawls into bed. As she talks to herself, the family exits quietly.)

Zhang Chi Maybe I am just crazy. I am excited about the parade . . . and about making the dragon . . . and about working with Li . . . the tail doesn't sound like too much fun . . . but maybe . . . maybe . . . *(She falls asleep.)*

(GONG, the dragon, enters and looks down at sleeping ZHANG CHI.)

Gong *(Shakes her gently)* Hey, Zhang Chi! Wake up!

Zhang Chi *(Looking up at the dragon)* Who are you? What are you doing here?

Gong My name is Gong, and I am the most beautiful, ferocious dragon in all of China!

Zhang Chi *(Rubbing her eyes)* Am I dreaming? Can there really be a dragon in my family's apartment? Should I yell for help?

Gong I wouldn't if I were you. If someone should come in, I would have to leave and I will never be able to tell you what I came to tell you.

Zhang Chi You came to tell me something?

Gong Well, of course! You don't think I visit girls just to talk about books and movies do you? I am a dragon! I have fish to fry! And trees to toast . . . and knights to . . . to . . . burn up.

Zhang Chi What do you have to tell me, Gong? I'm very excited to meet a real honest-to-goodness dragon! Do you actually breathe fire?

Gong Sure! Watch! *(He inhales.)*

Zhang Chi Gong! Wait!

Gong I was only kidding. Just making sure you are really awake . . . I mean paying attention.

Zhang Chi So . . . what do you want?

Gong Tea!

Zhang Chi I can't serve you tea! I mean, what did you come here to tell me?

Gong Oh, yes, that. Sorry. I came to tell you that you're looking at this parade thing all wrong.

Zhang Chi Oh. You've heard.

Gong Yes, I've heard that you will be the lucky one to carry the dragon's tail!

Zhang Chi Lucky? How can that be! My friend will be at the head of the dragon, a place of honor!

Gong Listen to me, Chi. I am a dragon with a long beautiful tail. See it? I can fly over the treetops and I can sail through the air, but do you know what happens to me all the time? Every time I soar up, up and away, through the forest, over castles? Do you?

Zhang Chi No, Gong, what?

Gong I cannot make my tail fly as high or as fast as the rest of me! I try and try—but it always lags just a little bit behind. And do you know what that means? It means that I am knocking the tops off of trees, or knocking flags off of castles. Or worse, burning myself on fires that I've breathed! Ouch!

Zhang Chi Gong, you must be joking with me! Your tail doesn't keep up with the rest of you?

Gong That is exactly it! In fact—do you know how we came to be called "dragons?"

Zhang Chi No! How?

Gong Because that is what our tails are always doing! Draggin'!

Zhang Chi (*Laughing*) Gong, I don't know whether to believe you or not!

Gong Believe me, Chi, when I tell you that, as a real live dragon, nothing would please me more than to have someone to support my tail for me. Then I would be up and over the villages without harming a single tree! Except for the ones I burn up on purpose, of course.

Zhang Chi I think I'm beginning to get the idea . . .

Gong It's much more important that you and the other boys and girls work together as a team than it is for any one of you to get a lot of personal glory. Every one of you is necessary. And as for your part in the project—always remember, Zhang Chi: The end of the story is just as important as the beginning.

Zhang Chi I see, Gong. I've been selfish and silly. I'd be honored to be any part of such a mighty dragon.

Gong All right, Chi! That's the spirit. Now turn over and go to sleep . . . and Happy New Year!

Zhang Chi *(Snuggling down as GONG exits quietly)* Good night, Gong. Happy . . . *(She looks up but he has gone.)* New Year to you.
(She falls asleep.)

(ZHANG CHI's family re-enters and assumes morning activities in the house. Breakfast is being prepared, MR. ZHANG & MRS. PING are putting on their jackets and getting ready for work. ZHANG CHI gets out of bed and enters breakfast area, hurrying around to gather up her schoolbooks.)

Narrator The next morning, Zhang Chi had a completely different feeling about her honor. She couldn't wait to make things right with Chen Li.

(He exits.)

Zhang Chi *(Entering)* Good morning, everyone! I don't have time to talk! I apologize to you all for being so silly about the dragon! I had a dream—sort of—and I know now that it's great to be involved at all! It's an honor, in fact! And the tail is very important, because it knocks down the tops of trees! And I must hurry to see Li and tell her how sorry I am before school starts! Goodbye! I'll see you all later!

(She exits. A pause, then:)

Grandma Chih-Chien See? I told you. Nuts.

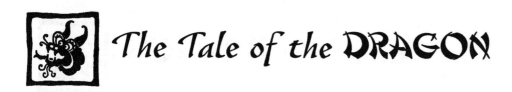

(As the family resumes their morning activities quietly and with subtle movements, ZHANG CHI and CHEN LI enter the courtyard area at the same time.)

Chen Li Chi!

Zhang Chi Li, my friend, can you ever forgive me? I was such a fool.

Chen Li I did think you were not acting like the Zhang Chi who is my friend.

Zhang Chi Well, that Zhang Chi is back. I will be honored, Chen Li, to help you build the dragon and to carry the tail proudly at the head of the parade!

Chen Li I've been thinking that we could trade, if that would make you happy.

Zhang Chi Oh, no, Li. You deserve to carry the head, my dear best friend. I'll help you build it!

Chen Li Oh, Chi! Yippee! We will have so much fun!

Zhang Chi Yes, Li, we will. It seems as if this "tail" has a happy ending—me!

(The girls hug and hurry off to school.)

(While the NARRATOR describes the activities associated with New Year's Eve, the families, including CHEN LI and her PARENTS, Mrs. Xin and Mr. Chen, silently act them out behind him.)

Narrator Before the girls knew it, it was New Year's Eve. The two families celebrated together at the Zhang's apartment and what a time was had! They enjoyed a feast featuring lots of fish, and a special vegetable dish called fatchoi— this sounds the same as the Chinese word for prosperity. There were special flowers and fruit—peach blossoms for long life and kumquat plants with little golden fruits. The Chinese word for kumquat sounds like the word for "gold" and "good luck." The girls were expected to stay up very late—a custom which they particularly liked! We Chinese believe that the longer the children stay awake on New Year's Eve, the longer lives their parents will enjoy. What fun the girls had on this particular New Year's Eve! They were given new clothing to wear the next day. This year, both girls were given something red, because red is a lucky color for festivals and celebrations in China. Finally, the children were given red and gold envelopes which contained Laisee or "lucky money." They wished their parents and grandparents Sun Nean Fai Lok, or Happy New Year! And most certainly it would be.

(The families hug and wave and part ways.)

Narrator Though they never wanted the evening to end, they finally had to go to sleep so that they could wake up and be ready to lead the parade the next day! The Chen family went home and the Zhang family went to sleep, and then—Chinese New Year dawned clear and bright and it was time to fly the dragon!

(Everyone gathers in the parade area. FENG LIBING, YU KAI, AND HUA DAN enter carrying the dragon.)

Mrs. Heu Everyone! Everyone! Gather around! You've done such a wonderful job on the dragon! He looks positively ferocious! What did you say his name was again?

ALL CHILDREN ON THE DRAGON TEAM
Gong!

Mrs. Heu Gong, yes, of course. Gong looks ready to fly. Everyone take your positions . . . Chen Li, you're at the front—the others in the middle—and you, Zhang Chi, take your position at the tail!

(The boys and girls do this.)

Zhang Chi With pleasure!

(GONG, appears to ZHANG CHI and catches her eye. In all the excitement, no one else seems to notice him.)

Gong Pssst! Chi!

Zhang Chi Gong!

Gong *(Lifting up his own tail)* Don't forgot to hold up your end of the bargain!

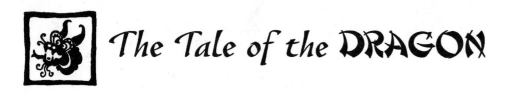

Zhang Chi Not a problem!

(He gives her the "thumbs up" sign and exits.)

Mrs. Heu Now, all the other performers line up!

(The other boys and girls line up, performing martial arts as they go, or beating on their musical instruments or warming up as though to sing.)

Mrs. Heu Is everyone ready? All right, then, on we go!

(As the parade begins around the room, the NARRATOR speaks.)

Narrator Chinese New Year is a time of hope, of joy, of celebration of all the things that make life wonderful! To you and your family, we say Kung Hey Fat Choi, which means "May prosperity be with you!" and we invite you to come join in our parade! This is the end of the play, but remember: "The end of the story is just as important as the beginning." Join us, won't you?

(Everyone urges the audience up out of their seats, hands them streamers, banners and musical instruments, and a procession takes place—just in the room, or maybe down the hall, or down the street!)